The Audit Evidence Process

The Audit Evidence Process

David J Hatherly, FCA

Assistant Technical Director, The Institute of
Chartered Accountants of Scotland

Anderson Keenan Publishing

First published 1980

Anderson Keenan Publishing Ltd
Imperial Buildings
56 Kingsway
London WC2B 6DX

ISBN: 0 906501 16 4 paper
       0 906501 17 2 cased

Phototypeset by Galleon Photosetting
Printed and bound in Great Britain by
The Garden City Press Limited, Letchworth,
Hertfordshire SG6 1JS

Contents

Preface

As far as auditing is concerned, evidence is at the centre of the stage. This book has been written in the belief that, in general, auditing texts do not adequately study the process by which the auditor evaluates – as opposed to collects – audit evidence. The tendency has been to concentrate on the routines for the collection of evidence at the expense of a detailed analysis of the factors influencing quality. In particular, it is my opinion that there has been too little consideration of how the auditor's assurance is affected by the combination of evidence from different sources. This is a most important issue, since the auditor seldom relies upon evidence from a single source.

I started with a very simple logical framework, which was:

(1) To identify the basic principles of audit evidence evaluation; and
(2) To apply these principles to the evaluation of evidence typically collected by the auditor.

In attempting to follow this framework I quickly found that it was going to be necessary to tread ever so slightly and ever so gently onto new ground. I took this to confirm my view that there is, at present, a gap in the auditing literature. The consequence is that, whilst much of the book provides a conventional treatment of audit evidence, there are some sections which are of necessity unconventional or at least novel in their presentation of conventional ideas.

The book has been written in the context of the auditing standards and guidelines which have been recently issued in the United Kingdom. However, the questions to which it is addressed are relevant to a wide variety of audits of financial statements wherever they may be conducted. It is hoped that for the student this book will prove a valuable supplement to existing texts. For everyone else concerned with auditing I hope it might provoke further thought and discussion of the important questions relating to evidence assessment.

David Hatherly
Edinburgh

1 Introduction

'If our beliefs are to be anything more than mere chance or emotional feelings, they must be based on evidence of some kind. The hypotheses which we develop, whether in our ordinary, daily activities or in some type of scientific endeavor, become strong enough to justify belief in them only if they are adequately supported by evidence. Evidence gives us a rational basis for forming judgments.

Auditing is like other disciplines in this respect. The auditor requires evidence in order that he may rationally judge the financial statement propositions submitted to him. To the extent that he makes judgments and forms his "opinion" on the basis of adequate evidence, he acts rationally by following a systematic or methodical procedure; to the extent that he fails to gather "sufficient competent evidential matter" and fails to evaluate it effectively, he acts irrationally and his judgments can have little standing.'[1]

This book is about audit evidence. It sets out the basic principles of audit evidence evaluation and illustrates their practical application. It is through an understanding and application of these basic principles that the auditor obtains and evaluates 'sufficient competent evidential matter' in support of the audit opinion.

AUDITING AND AUDIT EVIDENCE

In order to place the audit evidence issue in perspective it should be realised that the problem of collecting and evaluating evidence is one of four major elements in the overall audit process.

The credibility of the auditor is built upon:

(1) The ability to *communicate* the audit opinion clearly to those who rely upon financial statements;
(2) The ability to identify *criteria* against which financial statements are properly judged or assessed;

(3) The ability to *collect and evaluate evidence* indicative of how the financial statements perform against the relevant criteria;

(4) The *motivation* to perform properly all audit functions.

If those who might rely on the audit opinion are given reasons to doubt any one of these four elements, then the credibility of the auditor is brought into question, and the value of the audit opinion may be lost. The process by which the auditor collects and evaluates evidence with which to judge financial statements is just one important element in the overall audit process. However, an important part of the auditor's skill is the expert evaluation of such evidence.

The four elements may usefully be combined to give the following definition of an audit:

> An audit is the process of adding credibility to financial statements through an objective and expert evaluation of evidence as to whether those statements meet specified requirements and communication of the result to financial statement users.

Motivation is represented by the need for the auditor to be 'objective and expert', and established criteria against which to judge financial statements are represented by the phrase 'specified requirements'. 'Communication' and 'the evaluation of evidence' are specifically mentioned in this definition. The evaluation of evidence is either stated explicitly or is implicit in all definitions of auditing.

A CRISIS OF CONFIDENCE?

In the United Kingdom in recent years there has been something of a 'crisis of confidence' in the auditing profession. Much of the criticism has followed the reports of Inspectors appointed by the Department of Trade or the Registrar of Friendly Societies, many of which have been critical, to a greater or lesser extent, of the auditors or the auditing profession. Many of the points raised by the Inspectors concern, directly or indirectly, the question of collecting and evaluating audit evidence. The following paragraphs provide a highly abbreviated summary of points concerning audit evidence raised by the Inspectors.

(1) The auditor taking a more limited view of the audit objectives than the Inspectors consider desirable

The Inspectors raise a number of issues which call into question the objectives of the audit. For instance, to what extent should the auditor be concerned that the accounts disclose window-dressing operations? (A question of disclosure.) To what extent should the auditors be concerned to establish that directors' expenses do bring benefit to the company and should therefore properly be authorised by the Board? (A question of authorisation.)

Before the auditor collects and evaluates evidence, the detailed objectives of the audit must be well established. A list of these 'detailed audit objectives' is suggested later in this chapter and includes 'disclosure' and 'authorisation'. However, there is still a measure of uncertainty in the auditing profession as to the nature of the auditor's responsibility with respect to some of these suggested objectives, including those of 'disclosure' and 'authorisation'.

(2) Failure by the auditor to obtain in support of the audit objectives, evidence which would be generally regarded as reliable

The Inspectors' Reports relate cases of failure to obtain what they consider adequate audit evidence regarding, amongst other things,
(a) completeness of recorded cash receipts
(b) validity of building society mortgage summaries
(c) verification of creditors
(d) apportionment of profits between group companies
(e) stocktaking
(f) provision for obsolete stock
(g) research and development capitalised
(h) valuation of overhead component of stock
(i) completeness of contingent liabilities

The remaining chapters of this book do not address these specific problems (i.e. what would constitute adequate audit evidence in each case) but they are concerned to introduce a general approach to the collection and evaluation of audit evidence which if applied to these cases should have avoided the inadequacy. This general approach to audit evidence evaluation is considered in the following stages:

(a) The basic principles of audit evidence evaluation (Chapter 2);
(b) The logical application of these basic principles to the process of establishing each detailed audit objective (Chapter 3: the audit evidence process);
(c) A detailed consideration of certain important steps in the audit evidence process (Chapter 4: internal control, and Chapter 5: substantive testing);
(d) An illustration of the practical application of the audit evidence process by reference to the audit of sales and debtors (Chapter 6).

(3) Evidence which might generally be considered by the auditing profession to be reliable, proving unreliable

Third party evidence is generally regarded by the auditing profession as being reliable and yet the Inspectors report at least two instances where this proved not to be the case:

(a) In one instance the Inspectors found that the Chairman and Managing Director of a company had persuaded third parties to prepare and sign false documents. These third parties included a hotel, a football club, a motor car distributor, an investment company and an estate agent. In each case the third party was influenced by the fact that the Chairman was an important customer or business contact.
(b) In another instance an incorrect bank certificate had been given to the auditors by a recognised bank.

Chapter 5 discusses the factors which determine the reliability and persuasiveness of evidence from third parties.

(4) Failure to review the overall effect and suitability of accounting policies

In another report, the Inspectors consider that the auditors failed to adequately review the cumulative effect of individual accounting policies upon the financial statements of a company. Furthermore they failed to adequately examine, by reference to cash forecasts, whether the 'going concern' concept was appropriate. This book is primarily concerned with the processes by which audit evidence is obtained to support individual figures in the financial statements rather than the processes by which the auditor reviews the financial statements as a whole. The principal elements in the auditor's review of the financial statements are, however, stated in Chapter 3.

(5) Failure to properly plan, control and record the collection and evaluation of audit evidence:

The Inspectors are critical of several auditors who had failed in one or more of the following respects:

(a) To consider internal control and its effect on the audit;
(b) To use adequately trained and supervised staff;
(c) To record details of audit work done and conclusions reached.

If there is, as many commentators have claimed, a crisis of confidence in the auditing profession then it is clear from this cursory look at the Department of Trade Inspectors' reports, that failure to collect and effectively evaluate 'sufficient competent evidential matter' has played a significant part.

A FRAMEWORK FOR AUDITING STANDARDS

In an effort to boost the credibility of the auditor, the external auditing profession has issued a set of standards and guidelines. These are not standards in the sense that there are, for example, building standards which specify that foundations must be so many feet deep and walls so many feet thick. The auditing standards and guidelines are educational documents, for the benefit of auditor and financial statement user alike, outlining the thought processes which the auditor must conduct. They do not necessarily specify that such and such an audit test must always be performed or that audit samples must contain a specific number of items. Auditing standards and guidelines attempt to capture 'the audit process'.

A framework for auditing standards is readily developed from the four elements of the audit process. Specified requirements for financial statements are contained in *accounting standards*. Without accounting standards there cannot really be an effective audit since the financial user may be unclear as to the criteria against which the financial statements have been assessed. The importance of the accounting standards programme to the auditing profession should not be underestimated. However, for those financial statements which are required to show a true and fair view, the auditor should not lose sight of the ultimate accounting standard, i.e. the true and fair view requirement, irrespective of what is stated in the detail of particular accounting standards. The requirement for the auditor to possess the right motivation gives rise to *personal standards*, covering such matters as professional ethics and education, including continuing (i.e. post-qualified) education.

The auditing standards and guidelines[2] cover the remaining two elements of the audit process. The way in which the auditor should communicate the audit opinion(s) is covered in *reporting standards*, and the way in which the auditor should seek audit evidence on which to assess the financial statements is covered in an *operational standard*. This book is concerned to explain the thought processes which the auditor should conduct in meeting the operational standard.

The Auditor's Operational Standard

The Auditor's Operational Standard[3] states:

(1) This auditing standard applies whenever an audit is carried out.

Planning, controlling and recording
(2) The auditor should adequately plan, control and record his work.

Accounting systems
(3) The auditor should ascertain the enterprise's system of recording and processing transactions and assess its adequacy as a basis for the preparation of financial statements.

Audit evidence
(4) The auditor should obtain relevant and reliable audit evidence sufficient to enable him to draw reasonable conclusions therefrom.

Internal controls
(5) If the auditor wishes to place reliance on any internal controls, he should ascertain and evaluate those controls and perform compliance tests on their operation.

Review of financial statements
(6) The auditor should carry out such a review of the financial statements as is sufficient, in conjunction with the conclusions drawn from the other audit evidence obtained, to give him a reasonable basis for his opinion on the financial statements.

There are five distinct elements covering planning, controlling and recording, accounting systems, internal control, audit evidence and review of financial statements. However, there are really two main issues:

(1) The requirement to plan, control and record; *and*
(2) The requirement to obtain relevant, reliable and sufficient audit evidence to support the audit opinion.

The study of the accounting system, its internal controls and the review of financial statements are a part of the means by which the auditor obtains relevant, reliable and sufficient audit evidence and could, in that sense, be regarded as sub-issues of the audit evidence requirement.

Distinguishing the operational standard from the operational audit

The definition of an audit suggested on page 2 of this chapter assumes that the auditor wishes to assess a set of financial statements. Those financial statements should, of course, reflect the operational efficiency of the business entity to which they relate. However, the auditor's opinion, which is communicated to the users of the financial statements, relates to those financial statements, and there is no audit opinion on the operational efficiency of the enterprise as such. The operational auditing standard describes the processes which the auditor conducts to collect and evaluate evidence necessary for the assessment of the financial statements, and is concerned with the auditor's own operating efficiency in collecting and evaluating such evidence. It is not concerned with the operating efficiency of the business enterprise. Should an auditor be specifically requested to make an assessment of the operating efficiency of a business enterprise (as opposed to an assessment of its financial statements), such a task is frequently described as an operational audit. Operational auditing is outside the scope of this book.

Detail Audit Objectives

A major factor influencing the audit evidence needed in order to judge whether financial statements meet specified requirements is the nature of those specified requirements. This book is primarily concerned with the question as to what audit evidence is needed in order to make the following judgments relating to individual figures within the financial statements, i.e. whether for transactions,

(1) Recorded transactions actually took place (validity);
(2) Transactions which took place were authorised (authorisation);
(3) Transactions which took place were recorded (completeness);
(4) Transactions which took place were recorded in the right time period (cut-off);
(5) Individual transactions were recorded at the proper monetary amount (valuation);
(6) Individual transactions were appropriately classified (classification);
(7) Within appropriate classifications, individual transactions were accurately added together and summarised (summation);
(8) Transactions were summarised to an appropriate extent (disclosure);

and whether for balances,

(1) Recorded assets and liabilities exist (existence);
(2) Recorded assets are owned by the enterprise and recorded liabilities are attributable to the enterprise (ownership);
(3) Assets and liabilities which both exist and are either owned or attributable to the enterprise are recorded (completeness);
(4) Recorded assets and liabilities were both in existence and ownership at the balance sheet date (cut-off);
(5) Individual assets and liabilities are recorded at the proper monetary amount (valuation);
(6) Individual assets and liabilities are appropriately classified (classification);
(7) Within appropriate classifications, individual assets and liabilities are accurately added together and summarised (summation);
(8) Assets and liabilities are summarised to an appropriate extent (disclosure).

This list of criteria against which to judge individual financial statement figures is referred to in this text as the *detailed audit objectives*. The way in which the auditor obtains reliable and sufficient audit evidence relevant to the satisfaction of the detailed objectives is referred to as the *audit evidence process*. The final section of this chapter discusses the relevance and emphasises the importance of the detailed objectives to the audit of a limited company incorporated under the Companies Acts, 1948 to 1976.

The detailed audit objectives are not generally the only objectives of an audit, and the audit evidence process described in this book does not, therefore, necessarily cover the entire collection and evaluation of evidence required in an audit. However, the detailed audit objectives (and hence the audit evidence process by which these objectives are established) are a vital part of virtually all audits.

OBJECTIVES OF THE LIMITED COMPANY AUDIT

For a limited company, section 14 of the Companies Act, 1967 requires the auditor to form the following five opinions (Figure 1.1):

(1) As to whether or not the balance sheet gives a true and fair view of the state of the company's affairs at the end of its accounting period, and whether the profit and loss account gives a true and fair view of the company's profits or loss for its accounting period. (True and fair view)
(2) As to whether the financial statements comply with the Companies Acts, 1948 and 1967. (Compliance with Acts)
(3) As to whether proper accounting records have been kept. (Proper accounting records)
(4) As to whether the financial statements are in agreement with the accounting records. (Accounts agree with records)
(5) As to whether all the information and explanations necessary for purposes of the audit have been obtained. (Information explanations)

If the auditor fails to obtain sufficient evidence necessary for purposes of the audit (i.e. opinion (5) is negative) the logical consequence of this is that the auditor must be unsure as to whether one or more of the other four opinions should be positive or negative. The Companies Act, 1967 does not follow through the logic of a negative fifth opinion and it is left to the audit reporting standards to pick up the issue of uncertainty caused by limited audit evidence. The Act does not appear to conceive of the possibility of uncertainty with respect to any of the audit opinions.

Although the auditor must form five opinions, the Companies Act, 1967 does not require the auditor to report opinions (3), (4) or (5) if the opinion is positive. If the auditor says nothing in the audit report about these matters it is to be assumed by the users of the financial statements that proper accounting records have been kept, that the financial statements are in agreement with the records and that all required information and explanations have been obtained. In effect, the auditor is reporting his opinion by not saying anything. It is a form of reporting by exception. Opinions (1) and (2) must always be reported.

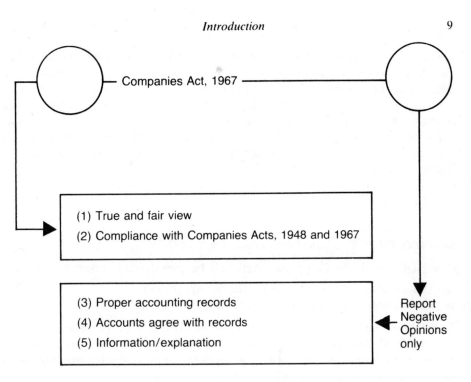

Figure 1.1   The objectives of the limited company audit

Detailed Audit Objectives and the Limited Company Audit

The detailed audit objectives are relevant to a wide variety of audit opinions including the five opinions required of the limited company auditor. Establishing the detailed audit objectives provides a *necessary, though not sufficient,* component of the audit work required for each of the five opinions.

True and fair view

In deciding whether a balance sheet or a profit statement gives a true and fair view it is necessary:

(a) To consider the quality of the individual figures appearing in the statements;
(b) To consider whether the cumulative effect and presentation of those figures taken together in the financial statements provides an overall true and fair view of the state of affairs and profit.

For the first of these requirements the auditor establishes the detailed audit objectives and for the second an overall review of the financial statements should be performed. The detailed audit objectives are a necessary prerequisite of the true and fair opinion. Each detailed objective should be established to the extent that it is material to the view given by the balance sheet or profit statement. The degree of assurance and hence the quality of evidence required for each detailed audit objective is determined by its relevance to the overall true and fair view objective.

Establishing the detailed audit objectives is not the only prerequisite of the true and fair opinion. In deciding whether a balance sheet or a profit statement gives a true and fair view it is also necessary to consider the cumulative effect and presentation of those figures taken together in the financial statements.

Compliance with Companies Acts, 1948 and 1967

Compliance with the Companies Acts may be considered in two parts:

(a) Compliance with the disclosure requirements; and
(b) Compliance with other requirements.

The detailed audit objective referred to as 'disclosure' requires the auditor to determine whether transactions, assets and liabilities have been summarised to an appropriate extent. If an 'appropriate' extent of summarisation is defined to incorporate not only

(i) The level of disclosure for the financial statements to show a true and fair view; *but also*
(ii) The disclosure requirements of the Companies Acts, 1948 and 1967,

then it follows that if the detailed objective 'disclosure' is established, an important (but not the only) element of compliance with the Companies Acts is established. There is a strong association between the detailed 'disclosure' objective and establishing compliance with the Companies Acts.

Proper accounting records

Section 12 of the Companies Act, 1976 requires that the accounting records of a limited company shall, amongst other things,

(1) Show and explain the company's transactions;
(2) Disclose, with reasonable accuracy, at any time, the financial position of the company;
(3) Enable the directors to ensure that the balance sheet at the end of the accounting period and profit and loss account for the accounting period give a true and fair view;
(4) Contain details of receipts and payments;
(5) Contain statements of stock held at the end of each financial year along with detailed stocktake listings;

(6) Contain statements of sales and purchases showing the goods and the buyers and (except for the retail trade) the sellers.

The detailed audit objectives relate to the individual figures in the financial statements rather than the accounting records. However, provided that the financial statements are in agreement with the records, then establishing the detailed audit objectives for transactions (including cash payments, receipts, sales and purchases) is relevant to the accounting records opinion. Similarly, establishing the detailed audit objectives for balance sheet items (including stock, creditors and debtors) is also relevant.

Agreement of the financial statements with the accounting records

This matter is investigated during the pursuit of the detailed audit objectives. For example:

(1) As part of the validity audit the accounting records are used as evidence to support the figures in the financial statements;
(2) As part of the summation audit the total of the accounting records of a class of transactions or balances is agreed to the related financial statement figure;
(3) As part of the completeness audit it is checked that all items per the accounting records are included in the relevant financial statement figure.

Information and explanations necessary for purposes of the audit

This is an interesting requirement since it is for an audit opinion, not on the financial statements or the accounting records from which those statements are derived, but on the quality of the audit evidence. The auditor must decide whether or not in his/her opinion all the information and explanations necessary for purposes of the audit have been obtained. In terms of the auditing standards 'has the auditor obtained sufficient, reliable and relevant evidence?' The results of the audit evidence process by which the auditor collects and evaluates evidence relevant to the detailed audit objectives is a major influence on the answer to this question.

SUMMARY

The following statements are drawn from points made in this chapter and serve to introduce the material which follows in later chapters:

(1) There is thought by many to be a crisis of confidence in the auditing profession.
(2) In an attempt to improve its credibility the auditing profession has issued a set of auditing standards and guidelines. The auditing standards cover

operational standards and reporting standards. This text is concerned to explain and develop the auditor's operational standard.

(3) More specifically, this text is concerned to explain the process (*the audit evidence process*) by which the auditor collects and evaluates audit evidence to support the individual figures within the financial statements.

(4) The criteria against which the individual figures in the financial statements are judged are termed in this text the *detailed audit objectives*.

The detailed audit objectives and hence the audit evidence process by which these objectives are established are relevant to a wide variety of audit opinions.

(5) In particular, they are an important sub-issue relevant to establishing whether financial statements show a true and fair view. They are also relevant to the other audit opinions required of the auditor of a limited company.

REFERENCES

1. Mautz, R. K., and Hussein A. Sharaf, *The Philosophy of Auditing* (American Accounting Association, 1961), p. 68.
2. The auditing standards and guidelines referred to in this text are those issued by the Councils of the following bodies:
   The Institute of Chartered Accountants of Scotland
   The Institute of Chartered Accountants in England and Wales
   The Institute of Chartered Accountants in Ireland
   The Association of Certified Accountants
3. Auditing Standard 101, *The Auditor's Operational Standard.*

2 Basic Principles of Audit Evidence Evaluation

The selection and evaluation of audit evidence to support the detailed audit objectives is the main subject matter of this book. Here we introduce the types of audit evidence which may be available to the auditor and provide a discussion of the basic principles which underlie the selection and evaluation of such evidence. An understanding of these basic principles is essential to an understanding of the audit evidence process as described in Chapter 3.

PRINCIPAL TYPES OF AUDIT EVIDENCE

The principal types of audit evidence may be catalogued as follows (examples are provided by reference to the audit of stock):

(1) *Accounting and other company records:* the balance on a stock account may provide evidence of the existence and valuation of stock and the balance on a bin card may provide evidence of stock quantities.

(2) *Physical observation:* the results of a stockcount by the auditor may provide evidence of the existence of stock.

(3) *Statements by third parties:* a 'we are holding the stock' certificate from a warehouse or other third party may provide evidence of the existence of stock.

(4) *External documents:* a supplier's invoice or price list may provide evidence of raw material prices.

(5) *Internal documents:* the enterprise's own costings may provide evidence of labour and overhead prices.

(6) *Recomputation:* recalculation of stock quantity × price multiples and the recalculation of the stock sheet additions may provide evidence of stock valuation and summarisation.

(7) *Representations by management:* explanations by management as to why they consider a stock obsolescence reserve to be appropriate may provide audit evidence of the valuation of stock. Such an explanation is normally included in a 'representation letter' received by the auditor from management.

(8) *Related accounts:* evidence which supports the purchases and sales of stock items may also support stock values since:

Opening stock + purchases − cost of sales = closing stock.

(9) *Post-balance sheet events:* sales of stock which take place after the balance sheet date may provide evidence of the existence of stock at the balance sheet date.

(10) *Expectations:* the budgeted stock figure at the year-end may be predictive of the actual stock figure.

THE QUALITY OF EVIDENCE

The first crucial concept which underlies the selection and evaluation of evidence is the concept of the 'quality' of evidence. To assess the quality of evidence the auditor must examine and assess the processes by which the audit evidence was created or generated. For this purpose it is instructive to consider three classes of audit evidence:

(1) Evidence created by processes largely under the auditor's control

If the auditor physically observes the existence of stock then the audit evidence (physical observation) so created is largely under the auditor's control in two important respects:

(a) The auditor can control the detail and accuracy of his physical count and hence vary the quality of evidence.

(b) The auditor directly experiences the process which creates the audit evidence and hence the quality of evidence can be readily assessed.

A further example of evidence largely under the auditor's control is recomputation by the auditor of arithmetic performed by the enterprise's staff in the first instance. Reliance upon expectations is to a certain extent under the auditor's control, since the auditor can select the sophistication of the analysis upon which the prediction is based. However, it should be remembered that the quality of the prediction is affected, not just by the quality of the analysis, but also by the quality of the information fed into the analysis. The quality of this information may be largely outside the auditor's control.

(2) Evidence created by processes largely under the director's control

The accounting records, internal documents and management representations should all be under the control of the enterprise's directors. To the extent that they are under the directors' control it is possible for the directors to manipulate such audit evidence in order that it gives apparent support to the financial statements. The majority of company directors are men of integrity, but the risk of director manipulation of evidence under their control does exist and is difficult for the auditor to assess. Clearly, the risk is greater for evidence which is immediately under director control (e.g. management representations) than it is for evidence, such as many internal documents, which is created or processed by the accounting system and hence is only indirectly under the control of the directors. However, even in the latter case the directors can arrange for internal documents to be created outside the routine accounting system, or documents created by the routine system can be suppressed. It should be stressed that in general the risk of serious director interference with audit evidence is low, but many Department of Trade Inspectors have reported cases of misleading evidence being provided to the auditor. In other words, although the risk of interference by the directors is low, the consequences can be very serious.

To assess the quality of evidence created by processes under the directors' control, the auditor must assess the integrity of the directors and the risk of director manipulation. The auditor should also assess the quality of the processes by which the evidence is created. To assess management representations it is necessary to know the reliability of the sources of information upon which management is relying when it makes the representation. Do they have first-hand experience of the issue upon which the representation is made, and, if not, have they made proper enquiries of a reliable source? To assess the quality of internal documents it is necessary to assess the quality of the accounting or other systems which have produced the document. How well organised and how well controlled is the internal system concerned?

The main features of audit evidence created by processes largely under the directors' control are:

(a) On the negative side, there is a risk of director manipulation which is difficult for the auditor to assess;
(b) On the positive side, the underlying processes by which the evidence is created, though not directly experienced by the auditor, are accessible to the auditor, who has the ability to question the basis of management representations and to investigate the enterprise's accounting and other internal systems.

(3) Evidence created by processes largely under the control of third parties

When the auditor relies upon statements from third parties or external documents, the underlying process which has created the evidence is largely under the control of the third party rather than either the auditor or directors. For example, when auditing the debtors of a business enterprise it is normal practice for the auditor to request the enterprise to write to a selection of its debtors (this selection being under the auditor's control) asking each debtor to write directly to the auditor confirming the existence of the debt. The quality of a debtors confirmation depends largely on the quality of investigation made by the debtor before writing to confirm the balance. If the debtor refers to his ledger account, then the quality of the confirmation depends upon the quality of the system which has generated that ledger balance.

The main features of audit evidence created by processes largely under third-party control are the reverse of those associated with evidence under director control. They are:

(a) On the positive side, there is relatively little risk of director manipulation, especially where the evidence passes directly from the third party to the auditor. However, there is always the possibility of a close relationship between the directors and the third party, which might enable the directors to pressure the third party into the supply of misleading evidence.

(b) On the negative side, the underlying processes by which the evidence is created are largely inaccessible to the auditor, who does not generally have the ability to question third parties or investigate their internal systems. This does not mean that third-party evidence is unreliable but rather that its reliability is not always known to the auditor. The degree of knowledge which the auditor has as regards the underlying evidence creation processes does vary depending on the third party concerned, and this question is considered further in Chapter 5.

The Quality of Evidence: A Summary

Figure 2.1 summarises the relative strengths and weaknesses of the three classes of evidence identified in this chapter by reference to the two questions around which discussion has centred:

(a) How susceptible is the audit evidence to manipulation by directors?
(b) How susceptible is the audit evidence to quality assessment by auditors?

Processes by which evidence is created largely under the control of:

	Auditor	Directors	Third Party
Susceptibility to director manipulation	Low	High	Medium
Susceptibility to quality assessment by auditor	High	Medium	Low

Figure 2.1

BALANCE AND CONSISTENCY

It is clear from Figure 2.1 that potentially the highest quality evidence is that which is created by processes under the control of the auditor. The Guideline on Audit Evidence makes this point as follows:

> 'Evidence originated by the auditor by such means as analysis and physical inspection is more reliable than evidence obtained from others.'[1]

Should the auditor then rely entirely upon such evidence? To do so would be very expensive, since creating this class of evidence involves a lot of the auditor's time. It is not clear from Figure 2.1 whether evidence created by processes under the control of third parties is preferable to that created by processes under the control of directors. The Guideline states that generally it is preferable:

> 'Evidence obtained from independent sources outside the enterprise is more reliable than that secured solely from within the enterprise.'[2]

The analysis of this chapter would not entirely support such a statement. However, it does support the idea that the auditor should, as far as possible, select a *balance* of evidence from across the three classes. Too much emphasis on evidence originated by the auditor is expensive. Too much emphasis on evidence secured within the enterprise leaves the audit susceptible to manipulation by the directors. Too much emphasis on evidence obtained outside the enterprise leaves the auditor susceptible to a mistaken assessment of the quality of the evidence.

The auditor is advised to seek evidence from different sources, and where this is done the *consistency* of the evidence must be investigated. The Guideline points out the significance of consistency as follows:

> 'When audit evidence obtained from one source appears inconsistent with that obtained from another, the reliability of each remains in doubt until further work has been done to resolve the inconsistency. However, when the individual items of evidence relating to a particular matter are all consistent, then the auditor may obtain a cumulative degree of assurance higher than that which he obtains from the individual items.'[3]

The effect of obtaining inconsistent evidence is to cause doubt and reduce audit assurance, whereas consistent pieces of evidence reinforce each other and improve audit assurance.

CONSISTENT EVIDENCE

It is useful to distinguish two possible effects of obtaining consistent evidence. Figure 2.2 illustrates the first possibility, which may be termed the *synergy effect* since the total audit assurance from two pieces of supporting evidence (A and B) exceeds the sum of the individual assurances obtained from A or B alone. In this case, the whole exceeds the sum of the parts. Figure 2.3 illustrates the second possibility, which may be termed the *diminishing marginal effect*, since the total assurance from two pieces of supporting evidence falls short of the sum of the individual assurances.

It is most important that the auditor is aware that, whilst obtaining consistent evidence always improves total audit assurance, the extent of the improvement can vary significantly. This significant variation can lead to either a synergy or diminishing marginal effect.

THE INDEPENDENCE OF CONSISTENT AUDIT EVIDENCE

If two pieces of supporting evidence were to be independent of each other in a strict statistical sense, the existence (or non-existence) of one piece of evidence would *not* affect the auditor's assessment of the likely existence of the other piece of evidence. This strict statistical independence is seldom the case in auditing.

Consider, for example, the following simplified example:

A stock purchase system involves the creation of a goods received note when stock is received. The goods received note is later matched with the purchase invoice and the goods received note and purchase invoice together generate a payment to the supplier.

In this example, the auditor has three pieces of evidence available to support the receipt of stock:

(1) A goods received note;
(2) A purchase invoice;
(3) A payment to the supplier.

However, given the interrelationships between the three pieces of evidence, as indicated by the systems description, the existence of a supportive goods received note will certainly affect the auditor's assessment of the likely existence of a supportive purchase invoice, and, in turn, the existence of a goods received note and purchase invoice together will significantly affect the auditor's assessment of the likely existence of a supportive payment to the supplier. Strict statistical independence does not exist in this example, and

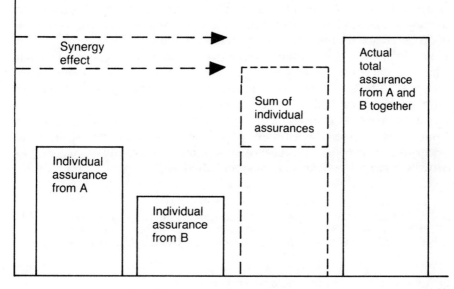

Figure 2.2   The synergy effect

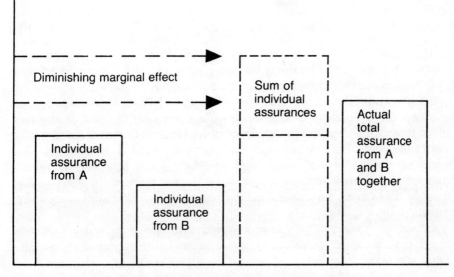

Figure 2.3   The diminishing marginal effect

independence in an audit evidence context is often a question of degree rather than absolutes.

When considering the effect of obtaining consistent audit evidence it is vital that the auditor considers the independence of the evidence, since it is this degree of independence which determines the extent of the improvement in audit assurance resulting from consistent evidence.

In particular, it is important to note that the synergy effect can only apply when the consistent sources of evidence are relatively independent of each other. In effect, this means that the processes which have created the different pieces of audit evidence should be independent of each other. As already suggested, relative independence is assisted by selecting evidence from across the three classes of evidence, since evidence created by processes under the control of different persons should be relatively independent provided that the people concerned are independent.

	STRENGTH	WEAKNESS
MANAGEMENT REPRESENTATIONS	from a source whose contact with and knowledge of the matter under consideration, is or should be, known to the auditor	from a source which may have an incentive to manipulate the evidence
OUTSIDE CORROBORATING EVIDENCE	from a source with no reason to manipulate the evidence	COMPENSATES

Figure 2.4

The auditor should not be surprised if evidence from non-independent sources is consistent! Obtaining further evidence from the same source can only have a diminishing marginal effect on total audit assurance.

To illustrate the importance of selecting a balanced cross-section of evidence from different independent sources, consider the role of management representations as audit evidence. Such representations are completely under the control of management, and the assurance derived from management representations *alone* is slight. In fact, many practitioners regard management representations as not giving any assurance at all, although this must be an extreme view unless management is regarded as untrustworthy or incompetent.

Consider, however, the position when evidence from sources outside management control corroborates those management representations. The auditor now has two independent and consistent pieces of evidence (Figure 2.4). Figure 2.4 shows that the weakness of management representations is compensated by the outside corroborating evidence's strong point (i.e. it comes from a source which has no reason to manipulate the evidence).

This then releases the auditor to give consideration to the management representation's great strength (i.e. it comes from a source which *should* have intimate knowledge of the matter under consideration. The auditor can question management to gauge whether such intimate knowledge actually exists).

The likely effect of outside corroborating evidence upon management representations is to create a synergy effect and an overall assurance level far greater than the sum of the parts. Of course, this synergy effect is reduced if the outside evidence comes from a source only partially independent of management.

INCONSISTENT EVIDENCE

The effect of obtaining inconsistent evidence is to cause doubt and reduce audit assurance. For example, in Figure 2.5, evidence A supports the financial statements and the assurance derived from A alone (without knowing anything about evidence B) is represented by block A. However, evidence B does *not* support the financial statements and the lack of assurance this causes

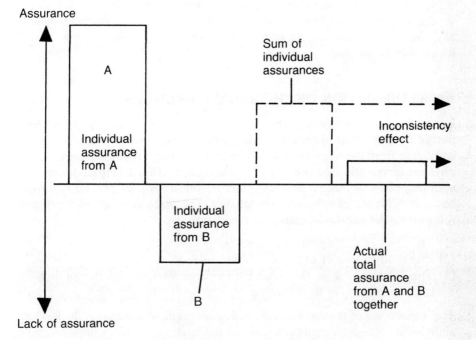

Figure 2.5   The inconsistency effect

(without knowing anything about evidence A) is represented by block B. When both evidence A and B are known, the auditor becomes unsure of the financial statements, since one source of evidence supports them and the other does not. Since the financial statements have the support of the higher quality evidence, the auditor still has some assurance in the financial statements (the actual total assurance from A and B is positive). However, this assurance is far less than the notional sum of individual assurances obtained by netting block B from block A. The difference between this notional total and the actual total assurance obtained gives rise to what might be termed an 'inconsistency effect'.

THE SUFFICIENCY OF AUDIT EVIDENCE

The Audit Evidence Guideline introduces the concept of sufficiency as follows:

'The auditor can rarely be certain of the validity of the financial statements. However, he needs to obtain sufficient relevant and reliable evidence to form a reasonable basis for his opinion thereon.'[4]

The auditor must decide the level of assurance required and audit evidence sufficient to provide that level of assurance must be obtained. There may be several options available to the auditor in the selection of sufficient evidence, and the next section is designed to illustrate the interaction of the factors which dictate the auditor's choice.

AN ILLUSTRATION OF THE BASIC PRINCIPLES

Let us suppose that the enterprise has stock at a warehouse run by a third party. Two available pieces of evidence of the existence of the stock are a certificate from the warehouse operator (A) and a visit to the warehouse plus physical observation of the stock by the auditor (B). Compared with the auditor's physical observation, the stock certificate is relatively inexpensive, but it is evidence of relatively low quality. The three key factors which are relevant to the auditor's selection of evidence are:

(1) The level of audit assurance considered *sufficient*;
(2) The relative *quality* of the available evidence;
(3) The relative *cost* of the available evidence in terms of the audit time required to obtain the evidence.

The importance of the second and third factors is dependent upon the level of audit assurance considered sufficient (the first factor), and this is demonstrated by Figure 2.6, where the level of assurance required is varied from low

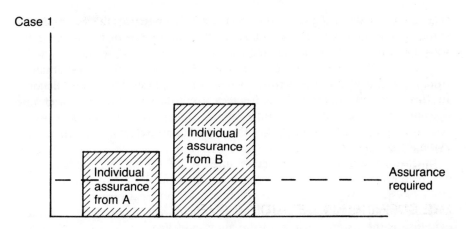

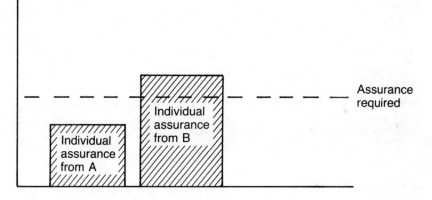

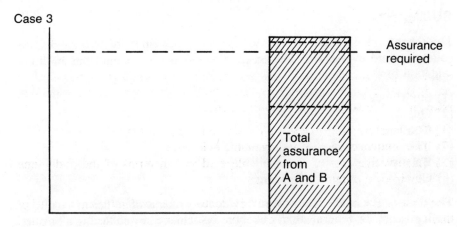

Figure 2.6   Three sufficiency levels

(Case 1) to medium (Case 2) to high (Case 3). In practice, the selection of a sufficiency level is largely influenced by the importance of the stock at the warehouse to the financial statements.

In Case 1 the assurance required is less than that which can be obtained from either the warehouse certificate alone or the physical observation alone. In this case, the auditor should select a certificate from the warehouse operator as being sufficient audit evidence since it is *relatively inexpensive*. At low levels of required assurance the crucial factor affecting the selection of evidence is *relative cost*.

In Case 2 the level of assurance required is greater than that which can be obtained from the warehouse certificate alone but less than that obtained from physical observation alone. In this case, physical observation by the auditor should be selected and the crucial factor affecting selection of audit evidence is the *relative quality* of the audit evidence.

In Case 3 the level of assurance required is greater than that which can be obtained from physical observation alone, and both sources of evidence are required. In the illustration the synergy effect is assumed since the two sources of the audit evidence are relatively independent.

Suppose the enterprise were to have not one, but ten warehouses. What effect would this have on the analysis? The effect is to make the analysis very much more complicated, and it is not suggested that the auditor does, or even should, go through a formal analysis each time he selects audit evidence. The auditor should, however, have knowledge of the key factors. In the ten warehouse case the number of options available to the auditor increases dramatically, but the factors behind the selection remain the same.

SUMMARY

This chapter has briefly discussed the basic principles of audit evidence collection and evaluation. The basic factors which lie behind the auditor's selection of evidence are:

(1) Sufficiency
(2) Quality
(3) Consistency
(4) Independence
(5) Balance
(6) Cost

The auditor seeks to obtain overall evidence which is of sufficient quality at the least cost. In general, this is likely to be achieved by collecting a balance of consistent evidence from independent sources.

REFERENCES

1. Auditing Guideline 203, *Audit Evidence*, para. 6.
2. *Ibid.*
3. *Ibid*, para. 7.
4. *Ibid*, para. 4.

3 The Audit Evidence Process

Chapter 2 identified ten types of audit evidence and three classes of audit evidence. By way of a reminder, these two analyses are repeated in Figure 3.1. The first analysis (types of audit evidence) focuses on the different forms which audit evidence might take. Such an analysis is helpful to the auditor who does not know where or how to *collect* audit evidence The second analysis (classes of audit evidence) concentrates on the underlying processes which create the audit evidence rather than the form which the audit evidence takes. Such an analysis is helpful to the auditor in the *evaluation* of the quality of evidence. This chapter introduces a third analysis (the audit evidence process). This third analysis concentrates on the *order* in which audit evidence should be collected and evaluated. It applies the principles of selection and evaluation of evidence outlined in Chapter 2 to the audit evidence available.

The steps of the audit evidence process may be summarised as follows:

DETAILED AUDIT OBJECTIVE

KNOWLEDGE OF BUSINESS

POPULATION STATISTICS

INTERRELATED ACCOUNTS

ANALYTICAL REVIEW

ACCOUNTING SYSTEM AND ITS INTERNAL CONTROLS

COMPLIANCE EVIDENCE

DETAILED SUBSTANTIVE TESTS

Each of these steps is considered in detail in this and subsequent chapters. The audit evidence process may be described as a logical sequence to the selection of audit evidence. The modern approach to the operational stage of the audit is to concentrate on identifying such an audit evidence process which can then be applied repetitively to different areas of the balance sheet (stock, debtors, cash, etc.) and different transaction areas (sales, purchases, cash receipts, etc.). A proper understanding of the audit evidence process,

Types of audit evidence	Classes of audit evidence
(1) Accounting records (2) Physical observation (3) Statements by third parties (4) External documents (5) Internal documents (6) Recomputation (7) Representations by management (8) Related accounts (9) Post-balance sheet events (10) Expectations	(1) Created by processes largely under the auditor's control (2) Created by processes largely under the directors' control (3) Created by processes largely under the control of third parties

Figure 3.1   Analyses of Audit Evidence

therefore, provides the key to the conduct of most areas of the audit covered by the Operational Standard. To understand why the audit evidence process is a logical sequence it is necessary to distinguish two properties of each of the steps in the process. These are:

(1) A step in the audit evidence process may have value in that its performance provides information which leads to a more efficient and effective performance of other steps in the audit process (a planning property).
(2) A step in the audit evidence process may have value in that its performance provides evidence of whether or not a financial statement figure meets a detailed audit objective (an evidential property).

Whilst both properties are present in all audit steps, in general those steps in the early part of the audit evidence process are those which provide valuable information for planning purposes and those in the later stages of the process provide valuable audit evidence. For example, knowledge of the business is important for audit planning purposes but of little value as audit evidence with which, by itself, to support the financial statements. The auditor should concentrate on that knowledge of the business which is easily acquired and yet is of great value in planning the proper scope of the later steps in the process. Detailed substantive tests such as a detailed examination of the valuation of a sample of items forming a financial statement figure is capable of providing high quality audit evidence. However, such an examination is time-consuming and therefore expensive, and should be used in response to the results of the earlier audit steps. For example, knowledge of the business may indicate the high-value items on which the auditor should concentrate the detailed substantive tests.

In a sense, the distinction between those audit steps which are valuable for planning and those which are valuable as audit evidence are irrelevant, since at the end of the day all steps in the process combine to provide the underlying logic supportive to the audit opinion. However, the distinction is useful as an explanation of the *sequence* in which audit steps are conducted.

DETAILED AUDIT OBJECTIVES

The detailed audit objectives are restated in Figure 3.2. The auditor should, through the steps of the audit evidence process, obtain sufficient audit evidence for each of these detailed objectives in turn. It follows that the auditor should consider the assurance required separately for each detailed audit objective, and there are at least three significant problems facing the auditor when selecting required assurance levels.

(1) There is a lack of knowledge amongst auditors of the levels of assurance which the users of financial statements expect the auditor to achieve from his evaluation of audit evidence.

This applies to all the detailed objectives.

(2) There are philosophical differences amongst auditors as to the nature of their audit responsibilities.

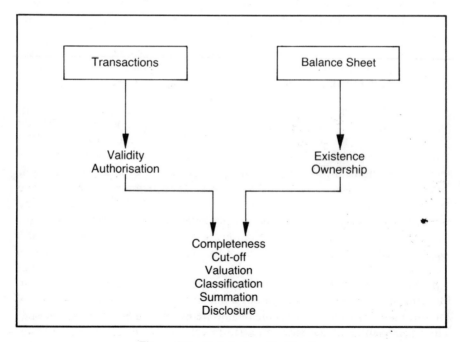

Figure 3.2   Detailed audit objectives

This can be most easily illustrated by reference to the *authorisation* objective.

Some auditors take the view that all transactions, whether or not they are properly authorised, should be similarly represented in the financial statements. According to this view, the question of authorisation is a matter for the directors and how they choose to run the business, and any comment by the auditors concerning a lack of authorisation would be a comment on the way the business is run rather than a comment on the financial statements. Following this line, the auditor does not require high levels of assurance that transactions are authorised.

An alternative view is that when purchases or sales are recorded in the financial statements and reported to financial statement users without comment, then the user is entitled to assume that the reported purchases or sales were properly authorised in accordance with appropriate authorisation procedures. Following this view, the auditor requires much higher levels of assurance with respect to authorisation.

(3) There may exist an expectation versus realisation gap.

It is useful to distinguish:

(a) The level of assurance which the financial statement user expects the auditor to obtain from the audit evidence (expected assurance); and
(b) The level of assurance which the auditor actually attains (realised assurance).

Even where the auditor can determine the expectation of the users, the auditor may not actually achieve the expected level of assurance for one of two reasons:

(a) The auditor interprets his responsibility as falling short of what a particular user or user group expects from the audit; or
(b) There is an inherent limitation on the quality of audit evidence available so that the auditor cannot achieve the expected assurance level.

In either case there exists an 'expectation versus realisation' gap. The *completeness* objective is particularly vulnerable to this problem. In many business enterprises, especially smaller enterprises, there is an inherent limitation on the audit evidence available to support the completeness of sales.

The Concept of 'Assurance'

The previous section has discussed the audit evidence requirements of the financial statement user in terms of the assurance which can be derived from the evidence. This assurance is directly related to the quality of the evidence. The requirements of the user can alternatively be expressed in terms of two other concepts: materiality and risk.

Materiality

The user does not need to know, for example, that *all* transactions are valid but rather that invalid transactions do not exceed a stated amount. This stated amount is termed the material amount. The concept of materiality is implicit in the statement of the detailed audit objectives.

Risk

The auditor can never be certain that a financial statement amount is not materially misstated no matter what audit evidence is obtained, and an element of risk is implicit in the audit evidence process. The user can express the audit evidence requirement by stating that the evidence must be of sufficient quality to ensure that the risk of material mis-statement is no higher than a stated level.

It follows that materiality and risk taken together, and assurance, are both expressions of an underlying audit evidence requirement. The relationships between the three concepts are illustrated in Figure 3.3. The basic idea is that *lack of assurance* resulting from a given level of audit evidence is measured by the area of a circle. The *materiality* and *risk* levels associated with the same quality of evidence are measured by the areas of the materiality and risk segments of the circle. Figure 3.3 symbolises the following relationships:

(1) Materiality and risk taken together are equivalent to 'lack of assurance': the equivalence of the concepts of materiality and risk on the one hand and 'lack of assurance' on the other is symbolised by the fact that, in each of the three circles, the materiality and risk segments taken together account for the whole of the circle.

(2) If the quality of evidence is held constant a reduction in risk can only be achieved at the expense of an increase in materiality levels: the inverse relationship between materiality and risk is symbolised by circles 1 and 2. If the quality of evidence is constant, the lack of assurance associated with that evidence is also constant, and this is symbolised by keeping the areas of the two circles constant. Since the risk and materiality segments must in each case account for the whole of the circle, it follows that the smaller risk segment (circle 2) must be associated with a larger materiality segment.

(3) An improvement in the quality of evidence can simultaneously lead to smaller amounts of both risk and materiality: the area of circle 3 is smaller than the area of the other two circles, symbolising a reduction in the lack of assurance associated with the audit evidence (i.e. higher quality evidence has been obtained). This smaller total area enables the areas of both the materiality and risk segments to be simultaneously reduced in circle 3 as against circle 1, symbolising that the levels of both materiality and risk are reduced.

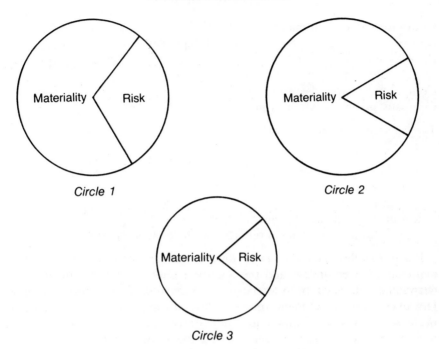

Figure 3.3   Assurance, risk and materiality

KNOWLEDGE OF THE BUSINESS

Acquiring knowledge of the business is the second step in the audit evidence process. It is not to be expected that the auditor will have as detailed a knowledge of the business as company directors and other members of the management team. Undoubtedly, over a period of time it is possible for the auditor of an enterprise to develop an extremely good knowledge of the business and its directors. It is sometimes argued that such knowledge is detrimental to the independence of mind and freshness of thought of the auditor. On the other hand, the better the auditor's understanding of the business, the greater the respect obtained from the enterprise's directors and staff and the greater the auditor's ability to plan the audit and understand the audit evidence. The auditor must tread a path which balances familiarity and independence.

The auditor who is conducting an enterprise's audit for the first time must find a substitute for the experienced auditor's slow accumulation of knowledge about the enterprise's affairs. The kind of knowledge which the auditor needs is knowledge of the enterprise's

Products – what is made?
Manufacturing process – how is it made?

Customers – who is it made for?
Raw materials and suppliers – what is it made with?
Plant location – where is it made?
Organisation and employees – who is it made by?
Competitors – who else makes it?
Company policies – why is it made?

Typical sources of such knowledge are:

A review of the permanent audit file;   ⎱ may belong to a
A review of prior years' audit working papers; ⎰ previous auditor
A scrutiny of trade and house journals;
Discussion with company directors and employees;
A tour of the plant and offices;
A study of previous annual reports and the annual reports of competitors.

These two lists are orientated toward the typical, medium sized, light manufacturing company, and the audit evidence process described in this chapter is illustrated by reference to a manufacturing business enterprise. However, the audit evidence process is equally applicable to other types of business: it is simply that illustration of the process by reference to a manufacturing company is likely to be the most readily comprehensible illustration for the reader.

Knowledge of the business embraces knowledge of the client's directors and what motivates them. If the auditor distrusts the directors then all evidence created by processes under the directors' control must be discounted by the auditor. This will undoubtedly leave a shortage of audit evidence to support key audit objectives such as completeness. In cases of serious distrust of the directors it is unlikely that the auditor can perform any satisfactory audit.

POPULATION STATISTICS

The auditor should obtain or create key statistical information about the accounting populations under audit. Such key information might typically include:

(a) A list of the individual items making up a financial total (item-by-item breakdown): clearly, such a list is essential if the auditor is to select a sample of items for substantiation in the detailed substantive tests.
(b) Where items forming an accounting population are serially numbered an important statistic is the range of numbers issued during the accounting period (population range): an auditor can easily select a random sample if there is a range (or ranges) of numbers forming the population. If the auditor selects a number and that item is missing from the recorded

transactions, the auditor has evidence relevant to the completeness objective, although the auditor should, of course, search for further evidence before concluding that an item *is* missing from the recorded population. It may be, for instance, that the particular number was never issued.

(c) An analysis of the accounting population total into sub-totals for different types of transaction or balance contained within the population (summary analysis by item type). A favoured analytical review technique amongst auditors is to break down (disaggregate) a financial statement amount into its principal components and to compare the amounts of these components with the equivalent figures last year. Clearly, such an analytical technique can only operate if the auditor is able to obtain appropriate disaggregations of the population.

(d) An analysis of the accounting population total showing the number and total value of population items within different item value ranges (summary analysis by item value).

The significance of summary analysis by item value

In Figure 3.4, Case 1 symbolises an accounting population with a large number of medium-value items and a small number of both low-value and high-value items (a 'normal' distribution). Case 2 symbolises an accounting population with a large number of constant value items and Case 3 a population with a small number of high-value items and a large number of low-value items (a 'skewed' distribution).

The form which an accounting population takes depends largely upon the type of business, e.g. a debtors population approximates to Case 2 if an enterprise (possibly a retail store) has a large number of small debtors and it will approximate to Case 3 if the enterprise (e.g. a supplier to Marks and Spencer) has one major customer and a number of much smaller customers. The auditor should test the shape of the accounting population for consistency with the knowledge of the business obtained in step 2 of the audit evidence process.

Later in the audit evidence process when the auditor performs detailed substantive tests, the sampling scheme employed by the auditor is influenced by the 'shape' of the accounting population.

In Case 2 the sampling scheme should select at random from the total population. In Case 3 the sampling scheme should, if it is to be efficient, give a greater chance of selection to the high-value items than to the low-value items. The effect of such a scheme is to divide the population into two strata (A and B). In Case 1 the sample scheme, if it is to be efficient, should effectively divide the population into three strata (A, B and C) giving a relatively high chance of selection to high-value items, a medium chance to medium-value items and a relatively low chance to low-value items.

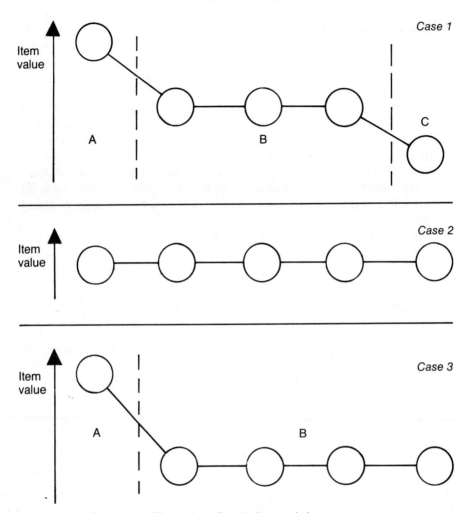

Figure 3.4   Population statistics

Thus the selection of an efficient sampling plan can be dependent upon knowledge of population statistics. The whole subject of what prior information is necessary before the auditor selects an appropriate sampling scheme for the detailed substantive tests is complex. Variable sampling plans do not, for instance, always operate satisfactorily on skewed populations (Case 3). Attribute sampling plans are of little use to the auditor for *substantive* testing unless items are of constant value (Case 2). The sampling plan of most frequent use to the auditor is monetary unit sampling, which automatically gives high-value items a larger chance of selection than low-value items. It can therefore cope with Cases 1 and 3.

RELATED ACCOUNTS

As a result of the double-entry accounting system there are many occasions where the same piece of audit evidence supports (or implies an error in) more than one financial statement figure. For example, suppose the auditor has evidence of:

(a) Goods shipped but not invoiced: this would result in incompleteness of debtors, non-existence of book stock, incompleteness of sales, and cost of sales.
(b) Sales recorded but goods not shipped: this would result in non-existence of debtors, incompleteness of book stock, invalid sales and cost of sales.
(c) Sales invoiced but not recorded: this would result in incompleteness of debtors and sales.
(d) Sales recorded in wrong period: this would result in cut-off errors for debtors, stock, sales and cost of sales.
(e) Invoicing errors: this would result in valuation errors for debtors and sales.
(f) Sales invoiced but not properly costed: this would result in valuation errors for stock and cost of sales.
(g) Sales made to bad credit risk: this would imply an authorisation failure for sales and a potential valuation problem for debtors and bad debts expense.

These examples of interrelationships concern sales, debtors, stock and cost of sales, but there are many other relationships in existence. Where there is a relationship between a transaction objective and a balance sheet objective the auditor has a choice: he can either put the main thrust of his audit into transactions testing, and in addition use his results as evidence of balance sheet objectives, or vice versa. The auditor should select the most efficient approach in the circumstances.

The auditor should be aware of the interrelationships between accounts both when planning the detailed audit work and when evaluating the results of the detailed audit work. Failure to take account of interrelationships at the planning stage will result in over-auditing, whilst failure to extract all the evidence contained in the results of the audit work is similarly inefficient. What is particularly dangerous is to take interrelationships into account at the planning stage but not at the evaluation stage.

ANALYTICAL REVIEW

In an analytical review the auditor attempts to predict one variable on the basis of an expected relationship with another variable (or variables) which is known to the auditor. The relationship between the variables is loosely described as a 'model' of the behaviour of the predicted variable. The difference between the predicted result and the actual result is a factor determining the extent of substantive tests and other investigations made of the actual result. The expected relationship between the variables is based on observation of the variables over a period of time. In a formal analytical review the relationship is determined from the observations by statistical regression techniques, whereas in an informal analytical review it is determined by subjective assessment. Where there is an absence of data over a period of time, the relationship between the variables can still be subjectively assessed but the quality of the review as audit evidence is much reduced.

Two simple illustrations where the relationship may be susceptible to regression techniques are as follows:

Illustration 1

The auditor attempts to explain sales in terms of cost of sales. For example, the auditor may observe sales and cost of sales for each of 48 months over a four-year period including the current accounting year. If 47 months show a stable gross profit percentage but one month in the present year shows a much lower gross profit percentage, then, on the basis of the gross profit percentage for 47 months, the auditor would predict a higher sales figure than the reported result for the 48th month. The auditor might concentrate his detailed audit work on the sales for the month in question but, before doing so, he should discover whether there is any ready explanation as to why the stable relationship was discontinued for the month in question.

Illustration 2

The auditor attempts to explain sales in terms of:

(a) Number of despatches; and
(b) A sales price index.

Again, the auditor would concentrate the detailed work on any periods for which the predicted result did not adequately match the reported sales figure, but not before ascertaining whether there are any other obvious factors not taken into account in the model but which might help to explain the sales figures for the months concerned. However, the auditor should examine whether the explanation offered has not already been taken into account in the model. For instance, consider the following circumstances.

There has been during the period(s) concerned:

(1) An interruption to supplies or production;
(2) A technological advance affecting price or the marketability of the product;
(3) A change in sales force or marketing arrangements;

(4) A government intervention affecting prices;

(5) A change in product mix.

Circumstances (1) and (3) should already be reflected in the number of despatches, and circumstances (2) and (4) should be reflected in the sales price index. Circumstance (5) provides the most plausible explanation as to why the model may have failed to predict actual sales. If the product mix changes, then the average sales value of a despatch is likely to change for reasons other than a movement in the sales price index. For example, if selling prices remain constant but the product mix moves toward a much larger number of smaller valued items, then the predicted sales figure (based on the number of despatches) will overstate the actual figure.

In the two illustrations given the model relies largely upon information internally generated by the enterprise. Cost of sales, number of despatches and possibly the sales price index (if produced by the enterprise) are all under the control of enterprise management. The auditor may, therefore, also wish to examine other models which make use of information drawn from outside the enterprise. Such information does have the advantage of being outwith the control of management but it may not otherwise be as good for prediction purposes as information from within. Nevertheless, the auditor may find useful informal models which relate sales, for sample, to one of the following:

(a) National disposable income;

(b) Industry sector growth;

(c) Sales of competitors.

Where information is drawn from outside the enterprise regression techniques are likely to be more difficult to apply due to a lack of frequency of the data (e.g. publication quarterly rather than monthly) and/or delays in the publication of the data.

The scope of the possible analytical reviews serves to emphasise the

	Accounting data	*Non-accounting data*
Enterprise	Cost of sales: management accounts	Number of despatches: despatch records
Competitors	Sales: quarterly interim figures	
Industry		Sales price index: central statistical office
Economy		Disposable income: central statistical office

Figure 3.5 Sources of analytical review information

importance of the auditor having a good *knowledge of the business*, the industry and the economy as a whole. The auditor may need available information about the enterprise (e.g. number of despatches), key industry indicators (e.g. sales price index), economic indicators (e.g. disposable income) and information about competitors (e.g. sales). The information needs, in this case, span both accounting and non-accounting data. Figure 3.5 summarises the main sources of information for analytical review purposes and gives some examples drawn from the illustrations of this section.

Using the enterprise's predictions

As an alternative to the auditor developing predictions, the auditor may use predictions made by the enterprise itself in the form of budgets or other forecasts. Where the auditor considers the enterprise's predictions to be made on a satisfactory basis:

(1) Its predictions for future time periods may form the basis of an assessment of the 'going concern exposure' of the enterprise; and
(2) Its predictions for past time periods may be used by the auditor for analytical review purposes, i.e. the basis of the analytical review is a comparison of budgeted figures and actual figures.

The Quality of Analytical Review as Audit Evidence

The strength of analytical review depends upon:

(1) The availability of suitable data from which to determine relationships. Those enterprises which have regular detailed management information are the most susceptible to sophisticated review techniques. In these cases, analytical review can have an important part to play in determining the scope of detailed substantive tests. For those enterprises, including many smaller enterprises, where there is a shortage of internally produced information for review purposes, analytical review can still play a significant role in determining the scope of detailed tests. However, the review must rely predominantly upon internal information produced annually for the annual financial statements and externally produced information. It is not generally possible to identify specific months for further detailed investigation.
(2) Validity of data. Where relationships between variables are established on the basis of invalid data, the analytical review may easily give misleading results to the auditor.
(3) The appropriateness of the technique used to determine the relationship between the variables. The more sophisticated and valid the technique used, the higher the quality of the predictions and hence the quality of the review.

It should be appreciated that the quality of evidence provided by, and therefore the assurance derived from, analytical review by itself is usually limited. Analytical review rarely establishes by itself that an accounting figure is 'right' or 'wrong' but merely indicates whether the figure looks 'right' or 'wrong'. The difference between the words 'establishes' and 'indicates' reflects a difference in the level of assurance obtained. However, the 'synergy' effect takes place when the indications of the analytical review are consistent with the detailed substantive test results and other audit steps.

INTERNAL CONTROL

An internal control may broadly be defined as any measure introduced by management of an enterprise to encourage the achievement of management's objectives. These objectives should include the production of financial statements which satisfy the detailed audit objectives and, for a limited company, show a true and fair view. The internal controls with which this book is most concerned are those which directly have an impact on the quality of the financial statements produced and are therefore of importance to the auditor.

Figure 3.1 lists ten types of audit evidence available to the auditor when forming the audit opinion upon the financial statements. The same types of evidence are available to the directors and staff of an enterprise when the financial statements are prepared. Since the directors of a limited company have a legal duty to produce a balance sheet and profit and loss account which give a true and fair view, any board of directors who seriously wish to discharge their responsibility will arrange for directors and staff to study high-quality evidence relevant to the preparation of the financial statements. *An internal control of relevance to the auditor exists whenever management or staff employ evidence relevant to the financial statement figures with the ultimate objective of ensuring that the financial statements give a true and fair view.* Wherever the preparation of financial statements includes the routine processing of large numbers of transactions, the accounting system should be designed to incorporate the routine employment of evidence of those transactions by enterprise staff.

Internal Controls and Accounting System Design

An individual operation performed as a part of the accounting system may fulfil one or both of two functions:

(a) The employment of evidence (an evidence utilisation function);
(b) The creation of new evidence or the modification of existing evidence (an evidence creation function).

For example, suppose the first operation in a goods inwards system is the issuance of a goods received note upon receipt of stock and the second operation is the matching and stapling together of the supplier's invoice and the goods received note, prior to the supplier being paid. In this example the first operation involves the creation of evidence of receipt (the goods received note). The second operation involves both the employment of evidence, since the goods received note and supplier's invoice are both studied, and the modification of evidence, since the goods received note and supplier's invoice are stapled together to create higher quality evidence of receipt for the next operation. The second operation fulfils both an evidence utilisation and evidence creation function.

It is important to recognise that an internal control exists at the point of the utilisation of evidence and not at the point of evidence creation. However, the auditor is interested in both functions, though for different reasons.

The utilisation function

It seems reasonable that if measures to ensure the true and fair view given by the financial statements have been introduced by the enterprise, then the likelihood of the financial statements being misleading is reduced. In other words, the existence of internal controls is itself audit evidence supporting the financial statements. A study of the evidence utilisation functions of the accounting system constitutes a distinct step (accounting system and its internal controls) in the audit evidence process. The important distinction between internal control and other steps of the audit evidence process is that other steps involve the utilisation of evidence by the *auditor*, whereas an internal control involves the utilisation of evidence by the *enterprise's staff*.

The same evidence may be utilised by the enterprise's staff in the first instance (internal control) and then by the auditor as audit evidence For example, the financial director may perform his own analytical review of the financial statements and this is then re-performed by the auditor. Another example of an internal control may involve junior staff. For instance, a clerk may ensure that for every stock purchase invoice there is a goods received note. The auditor may then re-perform this test for a sample of stock purchases. The crucial distinction between internal control and the other steps of the audit process is, therefore, not the nature of the underlying evidence but the fact that the enterprise's staff rather than the auditor is utilising the evidence.

The evidence creation function

In general, the auditor must study the processes by which any audit evidence is created or modified in order to assess the quality of such evidence. Where the evidence is created or modified by the accounting system the evidence creation functions of the accounting system must be studied. For example, in order to assess the quality of a goods received note as evidence of a stock receipt the auditor must assess the circumstances in which goods received notes are issued. Who has access to the blanks? Are they signed by the receiving department upon issue?

The auditor is interested in the quality of evidence created by the system, since such evidence is generally relied upon by enterprise staff elsewhere in the accounting system in the operation of internal controls and may also be utilised by the auditor in the detailed substantive testing.

The Quality of Internal Control as Audit Evidence

The quality of an internal control as audit evidence is determined by three factors:

(1) *The quality of the audit evidence utilised* by enterprise staff during the performance of the internal control.
(2) The *ability* of the enterprise's staff members to utilise the audit evidence concerned, and the *motivation* of the staff member to conduct properly the internal control and take any necessary corrective action.
(3) The *quality of the compliance* evidence obtained by the auditor to evidence that the internal control is being performed by the enterprise's staff.

Quality of evidence utilised

It is the quality of evidence utilised which determines the effectiveness of an internal control, *assuming that it is properly performed.* For an internal control to be effective it must utilise high-quality evidence *and* it must be properly performed by enterprise staff. If an internal control utilises high-quality evidence, evidence of its performance (compliance evidence) should be considered by the auditor. If an internal control utilises low-quality evidence then it is unnecessary for the auditor to consider either the ability and motive of the internal control operative or the availability of compliance evidence since little or no assurance can in any case be derived from the control.

Ability and motivation

There are many occasions where, because of their greater knowledge of the business and its systems, the enterprise's staff have a far greater ability than the auditor to utilise audit evidence. This is the potential strength of internal control as audit evidence, but what is the actual strength?

The auditor must acquaint himself with the capabilities of the enterprise's staff members who perform internal controls, and the auditor should consider whether each staff member's capabilities are commensurate with their duties. It is clearly impossible for low-calibre staff to perform high-grade internal control activities such as an analysis of standard cost variances or other analytical reviews. It is also undesirable for high-calibre staff to be assigned too many low-grade control activities such as matching invoices and goods received notes, since there is an obvious risk of demotivation. There are several other possible causes of demotivation which should also be considered by the auditor; notably, the staff member conducting the internal control may be effectively checking his own work or that of a close associate. This may cause demotivation, since any corrective action would involve the staff member or the associate in further work. This problem applies whenever the staff member is responsible for both the utilisation and creation of the same evidence. Moreover, the staff member who checks his own work does not bring to the internal control function freshness of mind or a second opinion where judgment is involved.

Quality of compliance evidence

It is quite difficult for the auditor to form a trustworthy judgment of either the ability or motivation of the enterprise's staff members. The auditor, therefore, generally requires further evidence that an internal control is being conducted as it should be. Such evidence is termed compliance evidence. Compliance evidence shows whether or not an internal control has operated. It may not, by itself, provide evidence that an internal control is effective since compliance is a *necessary but not a sufficient condition for an internal control to be effective*. To be effective, not only must there be compliance but the internal control must utilise high-quality evidence.

Evidence of compliance can take one or more of three forms:

(a) *Management representation*. Management responsible for the operation of the internal control and/or the internal control operative represent to the auditor (preferably in written form) that the internal control is performed.

(b) *Physical observation*. The auditor observes the internal control being performed by the enterprise's staff. Observation provides reliable evidence as to performance of the control at the time of observation, but not necessarily at any other time, since the internal control operative is more likely to perform the control function whilst under observation than at other times.

(c) *Inspection of written evidence*. The internal control operative produces a written report of the performance of the internal control, and this written report is inspected by the auditor. The written report varies from mere initialling of a document to evidence a check through to a full-scale report, stating work done, results, and resolution of problems encountered.

COMPLIANCE EVIDENCE

Management Representation

The availability of compliance evidence is under the control of management. It is possible that an internal control can operate satisfactorily from management's point of view without any written report to provide evidence of its performance. In such cases the auditor seeking compliance evidence is limited to reliance on a combination of physical observation and management representation. A management representation can only provide slight evidence of compliance unless independent corroborating evidence is available, in which case, as discussed in Chapter 2, the synergy effect may take place. It is doubtful whether physical observation can provide the requisite corroborating evidence, since the control operative can simply cease to perform the control once the observation ceases. In fact, the only source of suitable corroborative evidence may be the results of the detailed substantive tests. In these the auditor looks for evidence of the validity, authorisation, etc. (for transactions) and existence, ownership, etc. (for balance sheet items) of a sample of items making up the transactions or balance sheet figure. Good substantive test results are consistent with the *performance* of effective controls. If the only available compliance evidence takes the form of a management representation, the auditor derives little assurance from an internal control until the results of related substantive tests are known, at which point overall assurance in the relevant financial statement figure may be significantly increased through the synergy effect.

Compliance Tests – Inspection of Written Evidence

Where a written report of the performance of an internal control is available it is possible to devise a compliance test (consisting of an inspection of the written report) which provides a source of evidence of performance of the control independently of the substantive tests and of the management representation. If the auditor employs such compliance tests, then two 'synergy' effects take place. The first occurs provided that the results of the compliance tests corroborate the representations of management regarding the performance of the internal control concerned. This synergy effect is also conditional upon the compliance tests being relatively independent of the management representations. The second synergy effect takes place provided that the results of the substantive tests corroborate the compliance evidence provided by both the management representations and compliance tests. It is conditional upon the substantive and compliance tests being relatively independent.

The desirability of substantive and compliance tests being independent if they are to have a significant cumulative effect on audit assurance is sometimes not well understood by the auditor. Two criteria which can be used to investigate the independence of substantive and compliance tests are:

(1) An independent substantive test should be capable of evidencing whether a transaction is in error (i.e. invalid, unauthorised, etc.) irrespective of whether or not an internal control has operated upon the data;
(2) An independent compliance test should be capable of evidencing whether an internal control has operated upon a transaction, irrespective of whether or not the transaction is in error.

The two criteria can be illustrated by reference to the following common audit tests:

(1) The auditor re-performs the arithmetic of a transaction and compares the result with the valuation at which the transaction is recorded in the financial statements. (Audit test = re-performance.)
(2) The auditor checks for the existence of the initials of an enterprise staff member upon a document. The initials are recorded when the staff member performs an arithmetic check of the transaction recorded in the document. (Audit test = initials check.)

Re-performance

An arithmetic check by the auditor is generally more convincing evidence as to the proper valuation of a transaction than is knowledge of a similar arithmetic check by the enterprise. Even if the auditor knows the transaction to have been checked by the enterprise (the internal control has operated), re-performance by the auditor provides significant additional evidence of proper valuation. It is therefore capable of evidencing whether or not the transaction is in error, irrespective of the condition of the internal control, and is valuable as an independent substantive test.

Initials check

Many transactions are likely to be properly valued even without any arithmetic check by the enterprise, and it does not follow that a properly valued transaction must have undergone an arithmetic check. Therefore even if the auditor knows the transaction to be properly valued, a check for the existence of initials provides significant additional evidence that the arithmetic check was performed by the enterprise upon the transaction. It is thus capable

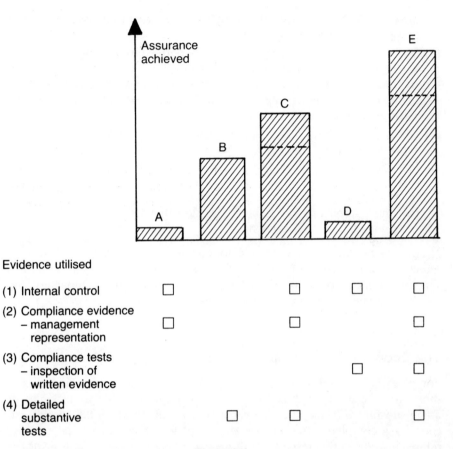

Figure 3.6

of evidencing whether an internal control has operated, irrespective of the substantive condition of the transaction, and is valuable as an independent compliance test.

Figure 3.6 illustrates the different levels of assurance achieved from different combinations of internal control/compliance evidence/detailed substantive test results:

(1) Block A represents a very low level of assurance in a financial statement figure derived from an internal control when the only form of compliance evidence is a management representation.

(2) Block B represents a level of assurance derived from substantive tests alone, without considering internal control.

(3) Block C represents the level of assurance derived when the evidence supporting block A and the evidence supporting block B is combined. It is assumed that the sources of evidence corroborate each other. The

area of the block above the dotted line represents the synergy effect (block C – (block A + block B)).

(4) Block D represents the level of assurance derived from an internal control where the only compliance evidence is in the form of an inspection of written evidence of performance. The assurance level ignores management representations regarding compliance and the results of the substantive tests.

(5) Block E represents the level of assurance derived when the evidence supporting block C and the evidence supporting block D is combined. It is assumed that all the evidence is consistent and that:

    (a) The substantive tests (supporting block C) and compliance tests (block D) are independent of each other; and

    (b) The compliance tests (block D) and management representations (block C) are independent.

The area of block E above the the the dotted line represents the overall synergy effect (block E – (block C + block D)), and the important point is that this synergy effect is only likely to be significant when the compliance and substantive tests are relatively independent.

The Economics of Compliance Tests

For the auditor there is always a trade-off between compliance and substantive tests. Time spent performing compliance tests could be spent doing substantive tests, and vice versa. The extent to which the auditor will consider a compliance test worth while depends upon its cost-effectiveness relative to substantive tests. Each of these factors (cost and effectiveness) are considered in turn. In some circumstances compliance tests are not cost effective and are ignored by the auditor. Two factors influence the *cost* of a compliance test:

(1) *Compliance tests require 'low involvement' with documentary evidence.* When they are available, compliance tests are relatively inexpensive for the auditor to perform since they only require a scrutiny of a written report, whereas a detailed substantive test requires evaluation of evidence by the auditor to substantiate individual transactions or balances. The latter is generally a more time-consuming occupation.

(2) *Compliance tests may be performed as a 'by-product' of substantive tests when both tests use common documentation.* Substantive and compliance tests may involve examination of the same documentation. For example, the auditor may wish to examine the initialling of purchase invoices by the enterprise as evidence of the enterprise's arithmetic check (compliance test), and he may also wish to recompute the arithmetic of invoices (substantive test). The sample sizes required for the two tests may

be different, but both tests require the auditor to be in possession of an invoice for each sample item. In such circumstances there is advantage in having as many sample items as possible common to both the substantive and compliance tests (i.e. the compliance sample is a sub-sample of the substantive, or vice versa). As far as the common items are concerned, the auditor requires the same documentation for both substantive and compliance tests, and hence the documentation necessary for both tests may be located as a single operation. Continuing the example, the auditor locates a purchase invoice included in both the compliance and substantive samples. He checks the invoice for the initials, recomputes and agrees the arithmetic, and then proceeds to the next common invoice. In such circumstances the marginal cost of performing compliance tests (substantive tests being in any case a necessity in most circumstances) is low.

It should be remembered that when compliance and substantive tests are actually performed simultaneously the *logical* order (as per the audit evidence process) is still

(1) Compliance tests, and
(2) Substantive tests.
It may still be necessary for the auditor to alter the scope of the substantive tests as a consequence of unexpected compliance test results.

Two factors influence the *effectiveness* of a compliance test:

(1) *The quality of the written report which evidences performance of the internal control*
The persuasiveness of such written evidence varies from that associated with mere initialling of a document to evidence a check through to the persuasiveness of a full-scale report stating work done, results, and resolution of problems encountered. Clearly, initialling a document provides low-level compliance evidence relative to a full-scale report. Unfortunately, the absence of persuasive written evidence is a frequent limitation on the effectiveness of compliance tests.
(2) *Where the compliance test is performed on a sample basis, the quality of the sampling strategy employed*
A high-quality sampling strategy should consist of two elements:
(a) *A representative sample.* One important point here is that the transactions should be selected throughout the accounting period, and should therefore be representative through time. The frequency with which an internal control is operated may vary during the course of an accounting period. When the enterprise's staff are under pressure from other directions the operation of internal controls may slip. In addition, the enterprise staff may change during the accounting period or control tasks may be re-assigned and different people

approach their internal control responsibilities with different degrees of diligence. For these reasons it is desirable that the auditor performs compliance tests throughout the accounting period. Other things being equal, compliance tests which relate to the whole accounting period are more persuasive of compliance throughout the period than tests which only relate to a portion of the period.

Another important point is that transactions selection should be representative of the variety of different transactions to which the internal control is applied.

(b) *A 'key item' sample.* A key item sample supplements the representative sample, and consists of those transactions which are considered by the auditor to either

(i) have a significantly greater than average chance of failing to undergo the internal control. For example, what happens when the control operative goes on holiday?

or

(ii) If in error, have a significantly greater than average chance of serious consequence to the financial statements. For example, high-value items may have a high chance of containing serious error relative to low-value items. The auditor is concerned that high-value transactions have undergone all relevant controls.

The auditor should, therefore, supplement his representative sample of transactions chosen for compliance testing with those transactions which have a high risk of non-compliance or a high risk of containing serious error. It is important to realise, however, that the sophistication of the sampling strategy can never compensate for a lack of quality in the written reports used to provide compliance evidence.

Compliance Errors

The auditor's reaction to errors discovered in the compliance testing is covered in the Guideline on Internal Controls which states:

'If the compliance tests have disclosed exceptions which indicate that the control being tested was not operating properly in practice, the auditor should determine the reasons for this. He needs to assess whether each exception is only an isolated departure or is representative of others, and whether it indicates the possible existence of errors in the accounting records. If the explanation he receives suggests that the exception is only an isolated departure, then he must confirm the validity of the explanation, for example by carrying out further tests. If the explanation or the further tests confirm that the control being tested was not operating properly throughout the period, then he cannot rely on that control.'[1]

DETAILED SUBSTANTIVE TESTS

The Explanatory Foreword to the Auditing Standards and Guidelines defines substantive tests as those tests of transactions and balances, and other procedures such as analytical review, which seek to provide audit evidence as to the completeness, accuracy and validity of the information contained in the accounting records or in the financial statements.[2] In the audit evidence process as described in this chapter:

(1) Substantive tests are subdivided into detailed substantive tests (i.e. tests of transactions and balances making up a financial statement figure) and analytical review procedures; and
(2) The detailed audit objectives to which the substantive tests are related are more comprehensive than the objectives of 'completeness, accuracy and validity' specified in the Auditing Standards' definition of substantive tests.

In the performance of detailed substantive tests, the auditor is not limited to an evaluation of evidence already studied by the enterprise's staff. The auditor can evaluate any available evidence, either internal or external, and whether or not it has previously been evaluated by the enterprise's staff,

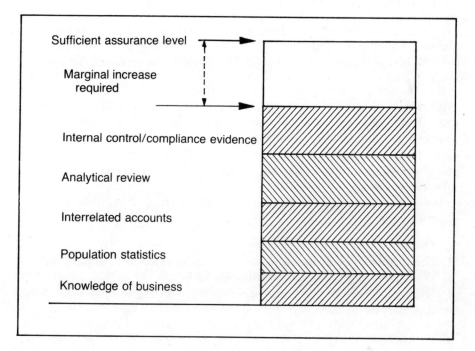

Figure 3.7

provided it is capable of substantiating individual transactions and balances in the sense that it contributes towards the satisfaction of one or more of the detailed audit objectives. Detailed substantive tests are normally conducted by the auditor by taking a sample of transactions or balances, and evaluating evidence, possibly from more than one source, in support of the sample items selected. Many types of audit evidence are on occasion employed to support the individual items, and this is illustrated in Chapter 6, which details substantive tests for sales and debtors.

The quality of evidence required from the detailed substantive tests (this is sometimes referred to as the 'scope' of the detailed substantive tests) depends upon the level of assurance achieved from the earlier steps of the audit evidence process. The detailed substantive testing, since it is the last step in the audit evidence process, must provide evidence of sufficient quality to take up the 'slack', and bring the assurance achieved to date up to the total level of assurance considered sufficient for each detailed audit objective.

An illustration of the increase in total assurance required from the substantive testing is given in Figure 3.7. The marginal contributions to total assurance made in this figure by the individual steps of the audit evidence process are illustrative only, and their relative sizes do change depending upon the circumstances. In general, however, the sequence of the audit steps in the audit evidence process is such that the marginal increase in assurance tends to increase as more audit steps are completed. This is because of

(a) The 'synergy' effect (assuming the results of audit steps are consistent with each other); and
(b) The higher quality evidence appearing towards the end of the process.

It is conceivable in theory, but most unusual in practice, for the sufficient assurance level to be reached without the need for any detailed substantive tests. This might happen in the audit of an enterprise with excellent internal controls and abundant information for analytical review purposes. For enterprises with few internal controls and little information for review purposes, the vast majority of total assurance will have to come from detailed substantive testing.

The marginal assurance achieved from the detailed substantive tests depends upon:

(1) The number of items in the sample;
(2) The quality of evidence employed to support individual sample items;
(3) The quality of the sampling plan employed;
(4) The consistency of the substantive results with the results of previous audit steps.

The relevance of these factors is discussed briefly in the remainder of this chapter and in more detail in Chapter 5.

Number of items in the sample: Statistical sampling plans are capable of indicating the extent to which assurance achieved responds to movements in sample size.

Quality of evidence employed: Even if a 100 per cent sample were tested substantively, the quality of evidence used would still provide a limitation on the quality of substantive testing as audit evidence.

Quality of the sampling plan: The more sophisticated and appropriate the sampling plan used to select sample items and evaluate sample results, the better the quality of evidence provided by the substantive testing.

A high-quality sampling plan should contain two components – a representative sample and a key item sample. A representative sample contains the characteristics of the population in the same proportion as the population. Of course, it is unlikely that any sample selected by the auditor will be truly representative, but provided that the sample is of adequate size and is selected by using an appropriate method, the risk of a significantly unrepresentative sample is low.

Three things can be said about the risk of selecting a significantly unrepresentative sample:

(1) The risk reduces as sample size increases. It reduces quickly at first but at high sample sizes it reduces much more slowly. Thus at small sample sizes a reduction in the risk can be achieved comparatively easily by extending sample size. At large sample sizes this is not so easy.
(2) The risk can be measured by using statistical sampling techniques.
(3) Irrespective of whether the risk is measured, the risk is, in fact, generally lower if the sample is selected at random rather than by judgmental methods.

Non-random samples may contain bias. The auditor may, for example, always pick the items which are easy to deal with; therefore such biases can be unconscious. Random number tables should be used to select random samples from numbered populations. Alternatively, a predetermined and systematic selection procedure might be used provided that it contained no known bias. For example, a sample of 100 may be constructed from a population of 4,000 by selecting every fortieth item, provided that there is nothing special or atypical about every fortieth item. Of course, the auditor can never be certain of this, and it is advisable to use random number tables as much as possible.

A further point on the construction of representative samples is that every item in the population should stand a chance of selection in the sample. It is all too easy for the auditor to omit a section of the population of items when selecting items for the sample. For instance, the auditor may select his debtors circularisations from a debtors' listing without checking whether the listing totals to the debtors' figure in the financial statements. The auditor may carry out the interim audit in October and ignore November and December transactions. Worst of all, the auditor may select his sample from April and December, and ignore the other ten months of the year.

The representative sample is supplemented by the selection of those transactions which the auditor considers to be key items. Such items are those which

(1) Have a significantly greater than average chance of being in error (invalid, etc.); or
(2) If in error, have a significantly greater than average chance of serious consequence to the financial statements (e.g. high-value items).

The representative component guards against the possibility of the population containing a significant number of errors. However, the representative sample cannot protect the auditor from the untypical isolated errors

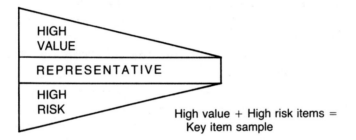

Figure 3.8   Desirable characteristics of a sampling plan

which, though few in number, have serious consequence to the financial statements. Such errors are, by definition, unrepresentative and atypical of the population as a whole. To guard against these errors the auditor must use his knowledge of the enterprise to concentrate scarce audit resources upon the high-risk and high-value items forming the key item sample. Whereas the representative sample is generally chosen at random and should be unbiased, the key item sample is chosen on the basis of the auditor's knowledge and is judgmental. The sampling plan, therefore, should include (Figure 3.8) a representative sample and a key item sample made up of high-value items and high-risk items. Such a plan makes use, in the high-value and high-risk items, of the auditor's knowledge and at the same time protects the auditor, through the representative sample, from too much bias based upon his knowledge.

The auditor should strike a balance between the representative and key item components of the sampling plan. Some statistical sampling techniques can assist the auditor to achieve a satisfactory balance. For example, some of the more sophisticated statistical sampling plans currently in use automatically strike a balance between the 'high-value' and 'representative' components. Stratified variables sampling and monetary unit sampling automatically bias toward high-value items. They do not, however, automatically give high-risk items a greater than average chance of selection.

The information on which to make an identification of high-value and high-risk items is contained in the results of the earlier audit steps. Figure 3.9

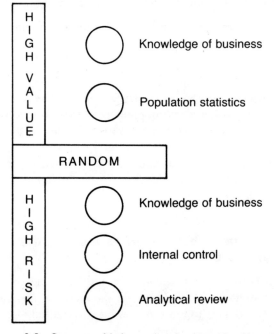

Figure 3.9 Sources of information for identification of 'high value' and 'high risk' items

indicates the principal sources of information, and the following examples are given by reference to the stock audit:

Knowledge of business: The auditor should have a good idea of the enterprise's most *valuable* supplies and products and of those items which are most at *risk* through pilferage, wastage or obsolescence.
Population statistics: These will identify the most *valuable* stock items.
Internal control: An assessment of internal controls will identify those stock items at greatest *risk* due to lack of control.
Analytical review: A study of, say, inventory turnover will identify those stock items at *risk* to obsolescence.

A final point on sample construction relates to the sample design. The auditor must have a clear idea of the type of errors he is looking for in his sample, and the sampling design must be equipped to do the job required.

The auditor does not look for a large fictitious sale in the small sales invoices. A sample designed to look for such errors is biased toward the large sale items, since, as far as such errors are concerned, it is these items which are at risk. Similarly, the auditor does not look for a failure to invoice a despatch by selecting a sample of sales invoices. A sample designed to detect such an error must be drawn from despatch notes. The way in which the sample is selected must be capable of satisfying the detailed objective of the audit test.

To summarise, the construction of the sample should recognise three points:

(1) A representative sample should be selected to provide assurance that there are not a large number of errors in the financial statements. The representative sample should be selected at random.
(2) The representative sample is supplemented by a 'key item' sample which searches for the untypical but serious errors. The representative and key item sample together form the total audit sample.
(3) The auditor must have a clear idea of the type of errors he is looking for in his sample and the sample design must equip the auditor for the discovery of such errors.

Consistency of the Substantive Results with the Results of Previous Audit Steps

Where the substantive results are inconsistent with the results of previous audit steps, the auditor will fail to obtain the marginal increase in assurance which was expected. This follows from what was quoted in Chapter 2:

'When audit evidence obtained from one source appears inconsistent with that obtained from another, the reliability of each remains in doubt until further work has been done to resolve the inconsistency.'[3]

In this case, the inconsistency is 'resolved' by obtaining greater assurance from the substantive results. The analysis of this section suggests that higher quality substantive results can be obtained in one of three ways:

(1) Improve the quality of evidence employed to support individual sample items: the first thing the auditor should do is to establish that the evidence being used is not misleading. This will almost certainly involve consultation with the enterprise's staff to see if there is any simple explanation as to the results being obtained by the sample tests.
(2) Revert to a more sophisticated sampling plan: the second thing the auditor should do is to establish that the sampling plan being used is appropriate. This will almost certainly involve an analysis of the underlying reasons behind any errors obtained in the sample and consideration

as to whether this additional information should be incorporated in the sample design. For example, if all the errors relate to one section of the stock the auditor may have new information of a 'high-risk' area, and the sample plan should select further items in this area to uncover the extent of the problem.

(3) Increase the number of items selected in the sample: if steps (1) and (2) above fail to resolve the inconsistency, the auditor is left with no alternative but to extend sample size generally.

THE REVIEW OF FINANCIAL STATEMENTS

If the auditor's ultimate objective is to form an opinion as to the true and fair view given by a set of financial statements then the audit evidence process as described in this chapter must be supplemented, as a final audit step, by an overall review of the financial statements. The true and fair view relates to the financial statements as a whole, and not to individual figures therein. The Auditing Standard states:

'The auditor should carry out such a review of the financial statements as is sufficient, in conjunction with the conclusions drawn from the other audit evidence obtained, to give him a reasonable basis for his opinion on the financial statements.'[4]

When the opinion on the financial statements is a 'true and fair view' opinion, a review of the financial statements is particularly important. The Auditing Guideline suggests[5] that when conducting such a review the auditor should determine whether in his opinion:

(a) The financial statements have been prepared using acceptable accounting policies which have been consistently applied and are appropriate to the enterprise's business;

(b) The results of operations, state of affairs, and all other information included in the financial statements are compatible with each other and with the auditor's knowledge of the enterprise;

(c) There is adequate disclosure of all appropriate matters and the information contained in the financial statements is suitably classified and presented;

(d) The financial statements comply with all statutory requirements and other regulations relevant to the constitution and activities of that enterprise; and ultimately whether

(e) The conclusions drawn from the other tests which he has carried out, together with those drawn from his overall review of the financial statements, therefore enable him to form an opinion on the financial statements.

SUMMARY

The audit evidence process provides a logical order in which the auditor should collect and evaluate evidence, since evidence obtained at an early stage in the process provides important planning information for the efficient conduct of the later stages of the audit. Some examples of this are given in Figure 3.10, to which the following notes relate.

(1) Knowledge of the business can indicate errors in the population statistics. For instance, a section of the business may be inadvertently omitted from population statistics, and, if so, the auditor should realise this from his knowledge of the business. The auditor should test the population statistics for consistency with knowledge of the business.

(2) Knowledge of the business may help to identify high-risk or high-value transactions for inclusion in the key item sample component of the detailed substantive test.

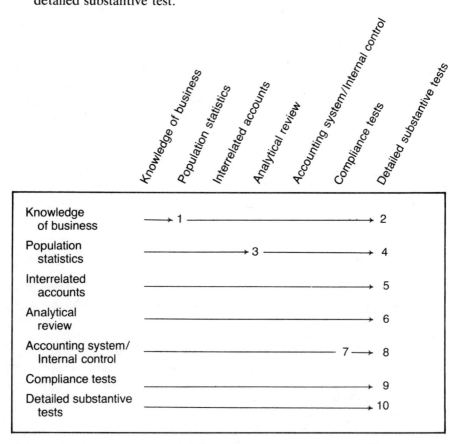

Figure 3.10   The audit evidence process: a logical order for the collection and evaluation of evidence

(3) Population statistics disaggregating financial statement figures permit the auditor to make use of analytical review techniques, studying movements in these disaggregated figures over time.

(4) Population statistics can assist detailed substantive tests in the following ways:
  (a) By providing a list of balances or transactions forming a total;
  (b) By providing an indication of possible high-value items for the key item sample;
  (c) By providing the range of serially numbered documents in issue from which the sample is selected.

(5) Interrelated accounts allow the auditor, for example, to test substantively for the validity of sales and cash receipts, and to use the results of these tests as evidence to support debtors. The auditor is, to a degree, given an element of choice between substantively testing transactions (sales, cash receipts) and balance sheet (debtors). A decision to stress the substantive testing of transactions has implications for the auditor's involvement with the accounting system/internal control stage of the audit process, since substantive tests of transactions normally use evidence processed or generated by the accounting system.

(6) Analytical review techniques can provide an indication of high-risk items or time periods for inclusion in the key item sample component of the detailed substantive test.

(7) The auditor will not conduct a compliance test unless his study of the accounting system shows that the internal control is capable of providing quality audit evidence. The accounting system will indicate the availability of evidence of compliance.

(8) The accounting system reveals the availability of evidence, processed or generated by the system, for use in the detailed substantive testing. A study of the accounting system operations helps the auditor to assess the quality of such evidence.

Those items which are badly controlled by the accounting system form a high-risk category for purposes of the key item sample component of the detailed substantive test.

(9) Those items which fail on compliance (i.e. those which bypass internal controls) also form a high-risk category for purposes of the key item sample.

(10) The representative sample component of the substantive test is generally conducted before the key item sample component, since a study of the errors in the representative sample may reveal new high-risk categories for key item selection.

REFERENCES

1. Auditing Guideline 204, *Internal Controls*, para. 16.
2. Appendix to the Explanatory Foreword to the Auditing Standards and Guidelines, para. 9.
3. Auditing Guideline 203, *Audit Evidence*, para. 7.
4. Auditing Standard 101, *The Auditor's Operational Standard*, para. 6.
5. Auditing Guideline 205, *Review of Financial Statements*, para. 2.

4 Internal Control

THE ACCOUNTING SYSTEM

This chapter identifies nine different types of operation which typically exist in a routine accounting system. A flowchart of twenty individual operations is introduced (see page 60), and this has been specially designed to illustrate one or more examples from each of the nine categories. It adopts the flowcharting method described in *Accountants Digest*, No. 32,[1] to which the reader in difficulties is referred.

The nine categories of operation are:

(1) Authorisation is required before a transaction is allowed to proceed (authorising).
(2) A source document is raised to record details of a transaction and to evidence its existence (raising source documents).
(3) Information is transferred to documents, directly or indirectly, from source documents (transferring from source documents).
(4) Two or more documents should contain the same information and the information is compared (comparing – details).
(5) Two or more documents should relate to the same transaction and the existence of both documents is checked (comparing – existence).
(6) An operation performed earlier in the accounting system is re-performed and the results of the two performances are compared (comparing – performances).
(7) Documents are pre-numbered on issue and are subsequently sequence-checked when filed (sequence – checking).
(8) Compliance evidence is created to evidence the performance of an internal control and the existence of the compliance evidence is subsequently checked (compliance testing).
(9) The physical location of documents is organised or reorganised (re-organising evidence).

Sales	Costing	Despatch	Sales Invoicing

(1) Sales order prepared by salesman in field

Sales order

(2) Approved and initialled by manager

Price/ cost records

(3) Checks for initials of sales manager

(4) Cost and selling prices entered and extended

(5)

(6) When goods despatched items are ticked and despatch note dated/initialled

Despatch note

(7) Details checked

(8)

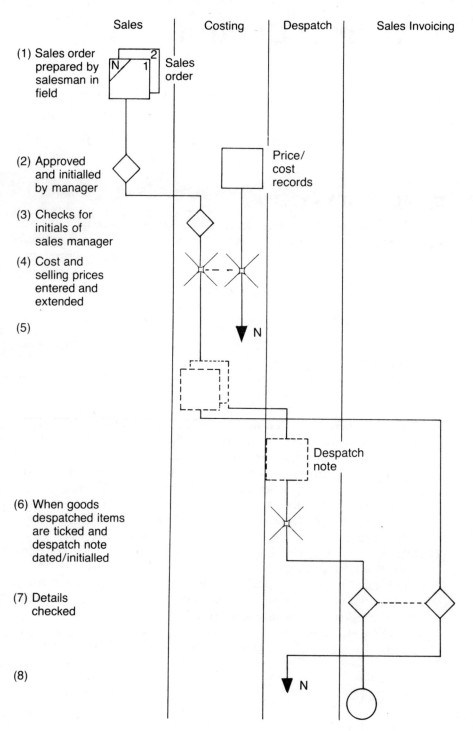

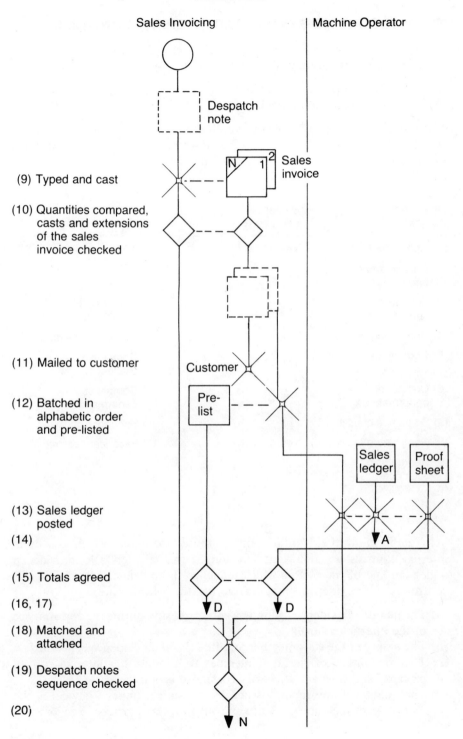

Sales Invoicing | Machine Operator

Despatch note

Sales invoice

(9) Typed and cast

(10) Quantities compared, casts and extensions of the sales invoice checked

(11) Mailed to customer

Customer

(12) Batched in alphabetic order and pre-listed

Pre-list

Sales ledger

Proof sheet

(13) Sales ledger posted

(14)

(15) Totals agreed

(16, 17)

(18) Matched and attached

(19) Despatch notes sequence checked

(20)

THE ACCOUNTING SYSTEM AND INTERNAL CONTROLS

As discussed in the previous chapter, each operation performed as a part of the accounting system fulfils one or both of two functions:

(a) An evidence utilisation function;
(b) An evidence creation function.

Those operations which involve the utilisation of evidence serve as internal controls. Using this criterion for the identification of an internal control it is found that the nine categories of operation yield seven categories of internal control (Figure 4.1).

Operation category	Evidence utilisation?	Internal control category
(1) Authorising	Yes	(1) Authorisation
(2) Raising source documents	No	
(3) Transferring from source documents	Yes	(2) Sound source documents
(4) Comparing details	Yes	(3) Comparison – details
(5) Comparing – existence	Yes	(4) Comparison – existence
(6) Comparing performances	Yes	(5) Comparison – performances
(7) Sequence checking	Yes	(6) Sequence checking
(8) Compliance testing	Yes	(7) Secondary control
(9) Reorganising evidence	No	

Figure 4.1

In addition to the identification of those operations which constitute internal controls an important function of this chapter is to provide an understanding of the factors which influence the potential of each internal control as audit evidence. In general terms, these factors are:

(a) The quality of evidence utilised by enterprise staff during the performance of the internal control;
(b) The ability of the staff member to utilise the audit evidence concerned;
(c) The motivation of the staff member to conduct the internal control properly and take any necessary corrective action;
(d) The quality of any reports issued by the staff member to evidence the utilisation of the audit evidence and any necessary corrective action.

In this chapter the specific application of these factors to each of the internal controls identified is discussed.

Authorising

Authorisation is required before a transaction is allowed to proceed. An example of this type of operation is given in the flowchart at operation (2). A sales order requires the approval of the sales manager before it is allowed to proceed. The sales manager uses evidence of creditworthiness in the form of his own past experience to decide whether or not the sales order warrants authorisation. Evidence, albeit informal, is utilised in this operation, and the quality of this internal control as audit evidence depends upon:

(1) The quality of the evidence utilised to determine whether or not the transaction warrants authorisation;
(2) The motivation of the staff member responsible for granting the authorisation;
(3) The quality of any compliance evidence.

In this particular example,

(1) How much experience does the sales manager have? What is the past experience of the enterprise with bad debts?
(2) Is the sales manager under pressure to increase sales? If so, what is his temperament? He may be tempted to increase sales for short-term advantage irrespective of the creditworthiness of the customer.
(3) The sales manager initials the sales order and this gives some compliance evidence of the performance of the authorisation procedure.

In this example past experience is used informally to establish the appropriateness of a transaction, since the decision depends exclusively upon the judgment of the sales manager. Past experience may be employed formally where, for example, no sales order is accepted from a customer who has exceeded the credit limit. However, it is likely that the sales manager or director would have the power to override any such formal rule.

Raising Source Documents

A source document is raised to record details of a transaction and to evidence its existence. Two examples of this type of operation are given in the flowchart:

(a) A sales order form is raised to evidence the existence of an order and to record its details (operation (1)); and
(b) A despatch note is raised to evidence the despatch of an order (operation (6)).

Such operations are designed to create documentary evidence, and the quality of the evidence created is determined by the circumstances in which it is created. The auditor should ascertain these circumstances through questions such as:

(1) Does whoever creates the evidence accept responsibility for it by signing or initialling the document?
(2) Is access to the blank documents restricted?
(3) Does whoever raises the evidence have direct contact and understanding of the transaction concerned?

In the case of the despatch note (operation (6)), for example,

(1) The despatch note is initialled by its originator.
(2) The despatch note is a copy of a sales order, and access to unused sales orders is not easy for those in despatch department.
(3) The despatch note items are ticked off as they are packed, indicating close contact between the originator of the documentary evidence and the transaction itself.

The view taken in this chapter of the creation of documentary evidence is that it does not, by itself, constitute an internal control since even the very best documentary evidence is useless if no one makes use of it. Therefore, operations of this type do not by themselves constitute internal controls although they do affect the quality of internal controls which utilise the evidence they have created. It is an example of the principle that an internal control arises not through the creation of evidence but through the utilisation of evidence. The importance of sound and reliable source documents becomes clear when the information contained therein is transferred to other documents and ultimately to the financial statements.

Transferring from Source Documents

Information is transferred to documents, directly or indirectly from source documents. Many operations within an accounting system involve the transfer of information. This may be transferred passively from one document to another without any formal scrutiny as to its reasonableness. In such a transfer there is a source document from which the information is taken, and an application document to which it is applied. Thus the operation involves both the utilisation of evidence (the source document) and the creation of evidence (the application document).

The quality of the application document as evidence depends upon both the quality of the source document and the accuracy of the transfer operation performed by the enterprise staff member. The accuracy of the transfer operation is in turn assisted by the clear presentation of information on the source document and a clear format for the presentation of information on the application document. There are several examples of this type of operation in the flowchart:

(1) Cost and selling prices are entered on the sales order from the price and cost records (operation (4)).
(2) The sales invoice is prepared from information contained in the despatch note (operation (9)).
(3) The sales ledger is posted from the sales invoices (operation (13)).

It may be considered that the transformation of a sales order into a despatch note (operation (6)) is a special case of this type of operation, with the source and application documents being, in fact, the same, and the transfer of information, therefore, being automatic.

It is to be hoped that the information applied, especially in the case of operations (4) and (9), does, in fact, attract some scrutiny from the person performing the transfer. However, this is not a formal part of the system, and may not be reliable as an internal control.

Although the information is merely transferred from one document to another and the evidence provided by the source document is not investigated or compared with other evidence, the transfer of information from sound and dependable source documents does, following the approach suggested in this book, constitute an internal control. The suggested approach is that an internal control exists whenever evidence of matters concerning the financial statements is utilised by enterprise staff. In this case, the evidence provided by the source document is relied upon without question.

The use of sound source documents has potential relevance to the detailed audit objectives of validity, completeness and valuation. If there is restriction of access to source documents, then the requirement to use source documents is relevant to the validity objective, since unauthorised personnel, at least, will be unable to initiate a source document into the system for a transaction which does not exist.

The relevance to the completeness and valuation objectives is best realised by considering the alternative to the use of formal source documents. If every time a transaction took place information relating to the existence and details of the transaction were transmitted to the accounts department by telephone, there would be a serious risk of:

(1) A transaction being overlooked by the accounts department (completeness); or
(2) The details of a transaction being incorrectly received by the accounts department (valuation).

There is not generally a compliance problem associated with this type of internal control, since the use of source documents by the enterprise can be readily observed by the auditor.

Comparing Details

Two or more documents should contain the same information and the information is compared. Such a comparison utilises evidence from more than one source and tests for consistency. The flowchart contains three examples of this type of operation:

(1) The details of the sales order and despatch note are compared (operation (7)).
(2) The quantities per the sales invoice and despatch note are compared (operation (10)).
(3) The control totals per the pre-list and proof sheet are compared (operation (15)).

The quality of any such comparison as audit evidence depends upon:

(1) The quality and independence of the evidence compared.
(2) The quality of enquiries made into any lack of consistency between the sources of evidence.
(3) The independence of the internal control operative from the sources of evidence under examination.
(4) The quality of any compliance evidence.

In the case of the comparison of sales order and despatch note, the following points are relevant to an assessment of the control as audit evidence:

(1) The sales order and despatch note ultimately originate from the same source, since the despatch note is a copy of the sales order. It follows that the two sources of information lack independence. Little is achieved by checking for the consistency of non-independent evidence except that it gives some assurance that the evidence has not been interfered with subsequent to its creation. In this example, assurance that the despatch department have not altered any of the details of the sales order is obtained.
(2) The comparison is made by 'sales invoicing', who are independent of both despatch and sales, the originating departments for the despatch note and sales order. This independence should ensure that the comparison is made by someone without involvement in the creation of the evidence.
(3) There is no compliance evidence available to evidence the performance of the comparison.

In the case of the comparison of the control totals per the pre-list and proof sheet the following points are relevant:

(1) The proof sheet is prepared automatically by machine during the debtors ledger posting. It therefore provides high-quality evidence of the total value of invoices posted.

(2) The pre-list originates from 'sales invoicing' and the proof sheet is prepared by the machine operator. The two pieces of evidence are therefore independent of each other.

(3) The comparison is made by 'sales invoicing', who are also responsible for the preparation of the pre-list. Thus there is non-independence of the person studying the evidence and one of the sources of that evidence. This is not ideal, but it is not a serious problem in this instance since the main purpose of the comparison is to check the activities of the machine operator, and the important requirement is that the person making the comparison is independent of the machine operator who is the preparer of the proof sheet.

(4) Some compliance evidence is obtained by checking on the existence of pre-lists and proof sheets.

In none of the three examples of this type of internal control given in the flowchart is there any indication of the quality of enquiries made into any lack of consistency between the pieces of evidence examined. The quality of these enquiries, and any necessary corrective action, is, however, a major factor determining the quality of the internal control. If no enquiries are made or no corrective action is taken, then there is no internal control. Once again, this is an illustration of the principle that an internal control arises through the utilisation and not through the creation of evidence. The auditor should seek evidence of enquiries having been made and corrective action having been taken. It is possible that such compliance evidence may take the form of a written report of problems encountered, enquiries made and corrective action taken. However, there are many cases where written reports are not forthcoming, and the non-availability of suitable compliance evidence is a frequent limitation on the value of this internal control *as audit evidence*.

Generally, a comparison of the details of documents is most relevant to the valuation and completeness audit objectives. For instance, a failure to reconcile control totals (operation (15)) may result from posting the wrong amount (valuation) or a failure to post an invoice (completeness). It may also result from the same invoice being posted twice (validity), or from incorrectly calculated control totals (summation).

Comparing Existence

Two or more documents should relate to the same transaction, and the existence of both documents is checked. This differs from the previous type of operation since the member of staff merely checks for the existence of all documents which should relate to the same transaction, and does not check that the detail of the documents agrees. Nevertheless, this type of operation may be regarded as a special case of the previous operation, and the factors which determine its quality as audit evidence are the same, i.e.:

(1) The quality of each of the documents as evidence of the existence of a transaction;
(2) The independence of the sources of the documents from each other;
(3) The independence of the person matching the documents from the creation of the documents;
(4) The quality of any enquiries into unmatched documents.

The operation is primarily concerned with existence. Non-existence of a document or record may indicate

(1) Incomplete financial statements (completeness); or
(2) Non-existent transactions recorded in financial statements (validity).

The flowchart contains one example of this type of operation. The sales invoice and despatch note are matched and attached at operation (18). Non-existence of an invoice may indicate that the sales ledger is incomplete, since a sales invoice may not have been raised or may not have been posted. Of course, it is not conclusive evidence of incompleteness, and further evidence would have to be obtained by the control operative to establish the position. For example, further enquiries may reveal that the sales invoice relating to the despatch has, in fact, been posted to the sales ledger but is missing. Non-existence of a despatch note corresponding to a sales invoice may indicate that a sales invoice has been raised when no despatch took place, i.e. it could be an invalid sale. Again, further enquiries should be made by the control operative to establish whether this is the case.

Useful compliance evidence is usually available for this type of operation. The existence of a file containing matched invoices and despatch notes stapled together and the existence of files for unmatched invoices and/or unmatched despatches all help to provide evidence that the matching process is being performed. However, the existence of old unmatched invoices or despatches may indicate that suitable enquiries are not being made, or are not being made promptly.

Comparison Re-performance

An operation performed earlier in the accounting system is re-performed, and the results of the two performances are compared. The quality of such an internal control is highly sensitive to the ability and motivation of the internal control operative. In this case the operative not only evaluates the evidence by comparing the two results but also creates one of the sources of evidence by re-performance. Motivation of the control operative is likely to improve when the operative is independent of the original performance, i.e. performance and re-performance are independent.

An example of this type of operation is given in the flowchart at operation (10), where the casts and extensions of the sales invoice are checked. In this case, the check is performed by sales invoicing, who were also responsible for the original casting of the sales invoice. Hence performance and re-performance are not independent in this example.

For this type of operation some compliance evidence can be provided by the control operative initialling the document which is being checked. However, in the example given in the flowchart no such compliance evidence is available.

Typically, the internal control operates through the recomputation of a mathematical or analytical operation, the result of which is then compared with the original computation. This is most likely to be relevant to the valuation objective, as is the case in the example given in the flowchart. However, the internal control can also operate through the re-performance of a prior internal control and a comparison of the conclusions reached on each occasion. In this case, re-performance and comparison is relevant to the same detailed audit objectives as the original internal control.

A variation on re-performance and comparison as an internal control can be seen where the control operative does not re-perform in every detail but does so in a rough and ready manner, and uses this rough and ready result to establish the reasonableness of the original performance. This is sometimes termed a 'reasonableness check', and could possibly be regarded as a separate category of internal control.

Sequence Checking

Documents are prenumbered on issue and are subsequently sequence checked when filed. Numbers missing from the sequence may indicate incompleteness of the financial statements. The existence of documents in the file with numbers which are out of sequence may indicate an invalid transaction having been recorded. An example of this type of operation is given in the flowchart at operation (19), where the numerical sequence of the despatch notes is checked. In this example, a missing despatch note may indicate a failure to invoice a despatch (incompleteness). Alternatively, it might simply be a sales order for which the despatch has been delayed. An out-of-sequence despatch number might indicate an invalid despatch note (validity).

The efficiency of sequence checking is very dependent upon the extent to which documents issued sequentially are processed sequentially. If some sales orders, for example, are processed much more speedily than others, then the number of missing numbers in the despatch note sequence checking will be high, and enterprise staff will spend much time making further enquiries to establish that these missing numbers do not represent a failure to invoice despatches. The quality of sequence checking as audit evidence depends upon:

(1) The quality of these enquiries made by enterprise staff into missing numbers and out of sequence numbers; and
(2) The quality of any compliance evidence to evidence the performance of the sequence check and any consequent enquiries made.

There may be in existence written reports of the performance of the sequence check, to serve as compliance evidence. However, the existence of such reports is unusual, and the absence of suitable compliance evidence is a frequent limitation on the value of sequence checking by enterprise staff as audit evidence. In these circumstances the auditor may decide to re-perform the sequence test in order to provide evidence (substantive evidence) which contributes to the substantiation of the completeness and validity of the data.

Compliance Testing

Compliance evidence is created to evidence the performance of an internal control, and the existence of the compliance evidence is subsequently checked by enterprise staff. The quality of such a check as audit evidence depends upon:

(1) The quality of the original internal control;
(2) The quality of the compliance evidence of the performance of the original internal control;
(3) The independence of the person performing the check from conduct of the original internal control;
(4) The quality of any compliance evidence of the performance of the check (as opposed to the original control).

An example of this type of operation is given in the flowchart at operation (3), where the costing clerk checks for the existence of the sales manager's initials on the sales order. The following points are relevant:

(1) The quality of the internal control whereby the sales manager is required to authorise sales orders has been previously discussed, and is a major factor affecting the value of any check of the sales manager's initials as audit evidence.
(2) The sales manager's initials provide some compliance evidence of the performance of the authorisation procedure. The value of initials as compliance evidence is, however, limited.
(3) The check is performed by the costing department, which is independent of the sales department and the conduct of the original internal control.
(4) No compliance evidence is created to evidence the performance of the check by the costing clerk.

In general, any internal control (such as the example given in operation (3)) which involves a member of the enterprise's staff checking to see that another internal control has been performed is called a *second level, secondary or supervisory control*. A secondary internal control is relevant to the same detailed audit objectives as the original internal control whose performance it is designed to check.

Evidence Reorganisation

The physical location of documents is organised or reorganised. The most common example of this type of operation is the filing of documents either alphabetically, sequentially or in date order. Filing takes place in the flowchart at operations:

- (5) (price and cost records)
- (8) (sales orders)
- (14) (sales ledger)
- (16, 17) (pre-list/proof sheet)
- (20) (despatch notes/sales invoices)

It might also be argued that the mailing of the sales invoice to the customer (operation (11)) is a further example of this type of operation, since the physical location of the sales invoice is affected. The organising or re-organising of documents does not involve the creation of evidence but merely improves (or otherwise) the accessibility of evidence already created. It does not involve the utilisation of evidence and therefore such an operation is not an internal control.

A SUMMARY OF THE MAIN TYPES OF INTERNAL CONTROL AND THEIR PRINCIPAL FEATURES

Arising from the discussion of accounting system operations, this chapter has identified the following types of internal control:

(1) Authorisation is required before a transaction is allowed to proceed (authorisation requirement).
(2) Information is transferred to a document from sound and dependable source documents (sound source documents).
(3) Two or more documents contain the same information and the information is compared (comparison – details).
(4) Two or more documents should relate to the same transaction and the existence of both documents is checked (comparison – existence).
(5) An operation performed earlier in the accounting system is re-performed and the results of the two performances are compared (comparison – re-performance).

(6) Documents are pre-numbered on issue and are subsequently sequence checked when filed (sequence checking).
(7) Compliance evidence is created to evidence the performance of an internal control and the existence of the compliance evidence is subsequently checked (secondary control).

The principal features of these controls are summarised in Figure 4.2 which gives, for each type of control,

(a) The evidence typically employed by the control;
(b) The type of compliance tests which may be possible, depending upon the availability of compliance evidence;
(c) The detailed audit objectives to which the internal control may, depending upon the circumstances, be relevant.

Figure 4.2 serves, in fact, to summarise the analysis contained in this chapter.

INTERNAL CONTROLS AND DETAILED AUDIT OBJECTIVES

Figure 4.2 incorporates the relationship between internal control categories and detailed audit objectives, but this relationship is shown more clearly in Figure 4.3. It is seen that several internal control categories can relate to the same detailed audit objective. For example, sound source documents, comparison of details, comparison-existence and sequence checking may all be relevant to the validity objective. Moreover, within each category there may be more than one internal control relevant to the validity audit objective. It follows that in assessing the assurance of the validity of transactions provided by internal control as a whole, the auditor should consider the interrelationship between, and cumulative effect of, all individual internal controls relevant to the validity objective. The same process of considering the cumulative effect of all relevant internal controls should be repeated for each detailed audit objective.

In essence, the same principles apply when considering the cumulative effect of controls as apply when considering the cumulative assurance derived from more than one piece of evidence supporting a proposition. This time, however, the auditor should consider, in addition to the quality of the evidence utilised in each control and the ability and motive of each control operative:

(1) The independence of the pieces of evidence utilised in the various controls; and
(2) The independence of the various control operatives.

Where, on the basis of these criteria, the internal controls may be regarded as independent, a 'synergy' effect is likely, and the cumulative assurance for

Type of internal control	Typical evidence employed by enterprise	Typical compliance tests by auditor	Possible detailed audit objectives
Authorisation requirement	Past experience	Observe initials on documents to evidence authorisation	Authorisation
Sound source documents	Source documents	Observe the use of source documents by the enterprise	Validity Completeness Valuation
Comparison of details	(1) Two or more documents (2) Results of enquiries into any lack of consistency	Study any written reports especially of any enquiries made	Valuation Completeness Validity Summation
Comparison – existence	(1) Two or more documents (2) Results of enquiries into any missing documents	(1) Scan file of documents stapled together (2) Scan file of unmatched documents and ensure no old unmatched documents	Validity Completeness
Comparison – re-performance	(1) Recomputation and comparison (2) Re-performance of internal control and comparison	Observe initials on documents to evidence the control or study any other written reports	(1) Valuation (2) Takes the objective of the original control
Sequence checking	(1) Serial numbering and sequential filing of documents (2) Results of enquiries into any missing or 'out of sequence' numbers	Study any written reports especially of any enquiries made	Completeness Validity
Secondary control	Compliance evidence of the performance of a prior internal control	Observe any initials on documents to evidence performance of the secondary control	Takes the objective of the original control

Figure 4.2

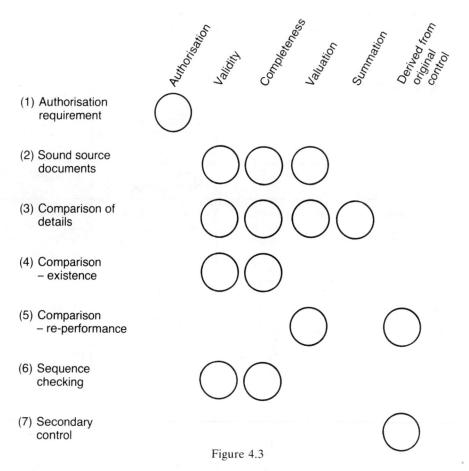

Figure 4.3

the various controls relevant to the detailed audit objective exceeds the sum of the separate assurances derived from each of the controls individually.

Where internal controls lack independence a 'diminishing marginal' effect is achieved.

As an illustration, consider the simple problem of combining two internal controls (A and B) both relevant to the same detailed audit objective. It is assumed that, by themselves, both A and B provide the same level of assurance (this is shown by the blocks A and B in Figure 4.5 being of equal size). The cumulative effect of the two controls is considered in four cases (C, D, E and F) which are summarised in Figure 4.4.

Case C

The evidence used in the two controls lacks independence from each other and so do the two control operatives. In an extreme case, the same evidence might be studied twice by the same person. (For example, a calculation might be checked twice by the same person.) In these circumstances the diminishing marginal effect is experienced, and block C (Figure 4.5) only shows a small increase in assurance over either block A or B and a lower total assurance than blocks A and B added together.

		Control operatives independent?	
		No	Yes
Evidence utilised in the controls independent?	No	C	E
	Yes	D	F

Figure 4.4

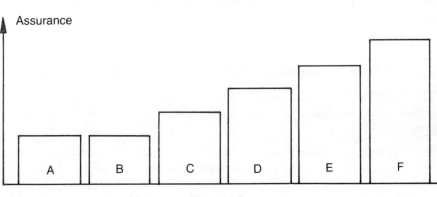

Figure 4.5

Cases D and E

In each of these cases the two controls lack independence in one key respect. In case D the evidence is independent, but the control operatives lack independence. As a simple example, the two controls may be operated by the same person. In case E the control operatives are independent but the evidence utilised in the two controls lacks independence. As a simple example, the two controls may use identical evidence but be operated by different people. It is not clear from the theory whether case D provides greater assurance to the auditor than case E. In Figure 4.5, block E is larger than block D, indicating a preference for independent control operatives, but the relative size of the two blocks must depend upon the circumstances.

Case F

The evidence used in the two controls is independent and so are the control operatives. In this case a 'synergy' effect is achieved and block F in Figure 4.5 is, therefore, drawn larger than the sum of blocks A and B.

The same ideas may also be applied to the problem of combining the assurance derived from an internal control (or internal controls) and substantive tests where both internal control and substantive testing relate to the same detailed audit objective. In this case, the substantive test operative (the auditor) and the internal control operative are automatically independent (assuming the auditor is independent of management), but it is still necessary for the auditor to consider the independence of the evidence used by the auditor in the substantive testing from the evidence used by the enterprise personnel in the internal control. When the substantive test involves the auditor in the 're-performance' of the internal control (i.e. the same evidence is utilised in the substantive test as in the internal control), then the marginal increase in assurance achieved by the substantive test may well be less than when the substantive test employs evidence independent of that used in the internal control.

Reconciliation with the Auditing Standards and Guidelines

The Auditing Standards and Guidelines[2] suggest the following as a classification and description of some of the types of controls which the auditor may find:

(1) *Organisation.* Enterprises should have a plan of their organisation, defining and allocating responsibilities and identifying lines of reporting for all aspects of the enterprise's operations, including the controls. The delegation of authority and responsibility should be clearly specified.

(2) *Segregation of duties.* One of the prime means of control is the separation of those responsibilities or duties which would, if combined, enable one individual to record and process a complete transaction. Segregation of duties reduces the risk of intentional manipulation or error and increases the element of checking. Functions which should be separated include those of authorisation, execution, custody, recording and, in the case of a computer based accounting system, systems development and daily operations.

(3) *Physical.* These are concerned mainly with the custody of assets and involve procedures and security measures designed to ensure that access to assets is limited to authorised personnel. This includes both direct access and indirect access via documentation. These controls assume importance in the case of valuable, portable, exchangeable or desirable assets.

(4) *Authorisation and approval.* All transactions should require authorisation or approval by an appropriate responsible person. The limits for these authorisations should be specified.
(5) *Arithmetical and accounting.* These are the controls within the recording function which check that the transactions to be recorded and processed have been authorised, that they are all included and that they are correctly recorded and accurately processed. Such controls include checking the arithmetical accuracy of the records, the maintenance and checking of totals, reconciliations, control accounts and trial balances, and accounting for documents.
(6) *Personnel.* There should be procedures to ensure that personnel have capabilities commensurate with their responsibilities. Inevitably, the proper functioning of any system depends on the competence and integrity of those operating it. The qualifications, selection and training as well as the innate personal characteristics of the personnel involved are important features to be considered in setting up any control system.
(7) *Supervision.* Any system of internal control should include the supervision by responsible officials of day-to-day transactions and the recording thereof.
(8) *Management.* These are the controls exercised by management outside the day-to-day routine of the system. They include the overall supervisory controls exercised by management, the review of management accounts and comparison thereof with budgets, the internal audit function and any other special review procedures.

Following the analysis of this chapter the only categories which should be regarded as internal controls in their own right are:

(1) Authorisation and approval.
(2) Arithmetical and accounting controls.
(3) Management controls in so far as these involve the utilisation of evidence (for example, the review of management accounts and comparison with budget).

Two key factors influencing the quality of these controls are:

(1) The ability and motive of the control operative, and
(2) The quality of the audit evidence utilised in the internal control.

Those matters listed in the Auditing Standards and Guidelines as types of internal control, but not regarded by this author as internal controls in their own right, are seen as matters which influence these two key factors.

Organisational controls, the quality of personnel and supervision all affect the ability and motive of control operatives. Physical controls affect the quality of source documents recording the movement of assets and hence they affect the quality of internal controls using those source documents. For example, restriction of access to physical assets considerably reduces the risk of assets being moved without appropriate documentation being raised. Segregation of duties may affect either the motive of control operatives or the quality of evidence utilised in an internal control, depending on the type of segregation of duties present.

Horizontal segregation of duties

Suppose evidence A is created to witness an underlying event and evidence A is used later in the performance of an internal control. In general, if the internal control operative is independent of the evidence creation, then the process of evidence creation is given a degree of scrutiny and inspection by the control operative which is lacking if the operative and the creator of the

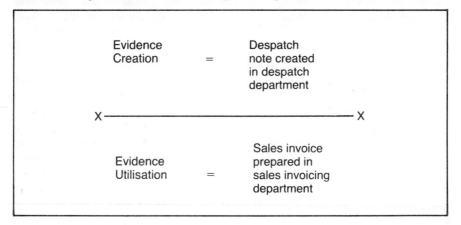

Figure 4.6

evidence are one and the same. If evidence utilisation and creation are independent then there is what might be termed *horizontal* segregation of duties. In Figure 4.6 the *horizontal* line xx represents a 'functional divide' between evidence creation (for example, the creation of a despatch note in despatch department) and evidence utilised (for example, the preparation of a sales invoice in the sales invoicing department using information contained on the despatch note).

In terms of the flowcharting technique described in *Accountants Digest*, No. 32, horizontal segregation of duties appears as shown in Figure 4.7. This segregation of duties improves the motive of the internal control operative.

Vertical segregation of duties

Suppose that *two* pieces of evidence (A and B) are independently prepared to witness the same underlying event. Such independent preparation is achieved if the creation of evidence A and evidence B is allocated to

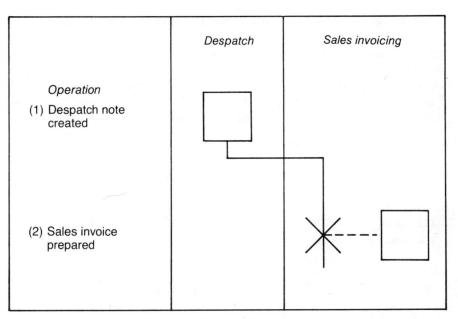

Figure 4.7

independent individuals and, if such is the case, it may be termed a *vertical* segregation of duties. In Figure 4.8 the *vertical* line YY represents a 'functional divide' between the creation of evidence A (for example, a sales order prepared in sales department evidencing the existence of a valid sale) and the creation of evidence B (for example, a despatch note prepared in despatch department also evidencing a valid sale).

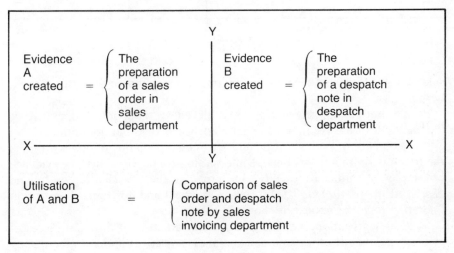

Figure 4.8

If both pieces of evidence are used and compared later in the performance of an internal control then, since the evidence comes from independent sources, the quality of evidence used in the control is likely to be high. If the utilisation of evidence A and B is by a person independent of the creation of both A and B then horizontal segregation is also present. (For example, in Figure 4.8, the line xx represents the fact that the details of the sales order and despatch note are compared by sales invoicing before preparation of a

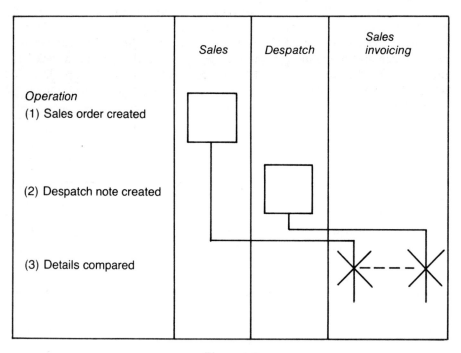

Figure 4.9

sales invoice. Sales invoicing is a department independent of both sales and despatch.)

Partial horizontal segregation is achieved if the control operative is independent of the creation of either evidence A or B but not both.

The existence of both vertical and horizontal segregation of duties provides the framework for a truly effective internal control provided that the evidence utilised is of sufficient quality. In terms of the flowcharting technique described in *Accountants Digest*, No. 32 vertical and horizontal segregation operating together appear as shown in Figure 4.9.

Vertical segregation (i.e. the independent creation of different pieces of evidence relevant to the same detailed audit objective) improves the quality of evidence available for subsequent internal controls.

SUMMARY

It should be recognised that a study of internal control provides limited audit evidence and is seldom capable of establishing by itself whether the financial statements are acceptable to the auditor. The quality of evidence provided by a study of internal control is, for example, in general less than the quality of evidence provided by substantive testing for the following reasons:

The 'people' problem: Any evaluation of internal control is susceptible to error because of the dependence of internal control upon the control operative. When the auditor evaluates a control he is evaluating the competence and motivation of the people operating the control, and this is inevitably a subjective process. Moreover, the task is made more difficult when either the people themselves, or the pressures under which they are operating, are not constant but are changing during the accounting period under consideration. The problem is complicated still further when it is considered that one of these pressures may be the pressure of senior management upon staff to allow override of internal controls. Thus the auditor is not only evaluating staff operating the controls but also the character and motivation of management. Although it is entirely necessary that the auditor should make such an evaluation it should be recognised that such an evaluation is subjective.

The 'compliance' problem: Formal evidence of compliance exists whenever the internal control operative issues a written report evidencing the conduct of the control procedure. The persuasiveness of compliance evidence varies from that associated with mere initialling of a document to evidence a check through to the persuasiveness of a full-scale report stating work done, results and resolution of problems encountered. Unfortunately, from the auditor's point of view, the issuance of formal reports by a control operative is in many cases considered unnecessary by management, and hence the auditor is left without evidence on the basis of which he can assert that the internal control is operating.

Neither the 'people' problem nor the 'compliance' problem apply to substantive testing, since with substantive testing it is the auditor and not the enterprise's staff who utilises and appraises the underlying evidence. Nevertheless, in spite of these problems a study of internal controls provides a valuable source of audit evidence supporting the financial statements *provided* that the operation of good internal controls is consistent with and corroborated by the results of the auditor's substantive testing. This chapter has

(1) Identified the principal categories of internal control;
(2) Given examples of specific controls from each category;
(3) Discussed the quality of each internal control category as audit evidence;

(4) Discussed the relevance of each internal control category to the detailed audit objectives;

(5) Demonstrated the principles underlying an assessment of the cumulative effect of internal controls and the cumulative effect of internal controls plus substantive testing.

REFERENCES

1. Accountants Digest, No. 32, *Flowcharting for Auditors* (Institute of Chartered Accountants in England and Wales, 1976).
2. Auditing Guideline 204, *Internal Controls*, Appendix, paras. 1 to 8.

5 Substantive Testing

SUBSTANTIVE TEST DESIGN

This chapter introduces a general approach to the design of substantive tests. Specific illustration of the application of this approach is given in Chapter 6, which discusses substantive tests appropriate to the audit of sales and to the audit of debtors. The overriding requirement of the substantive testing as indicated in the bottom line of Figure 5.1, is that the assurance *required* for each detailed audit objective is actually *achieved*. For each detailed objective some assurance will have been obtained from audit steps performed prior to the substantive testing. Hence, as indicated by the left-hand side of Figure 5.1, the assurance required from the substantive testing for a particular audit objective is the net of the overall assurance required and the assurance achieved to date from other audit steps.

The right-hand side of Figure 5.1 indicates, not necessarily in order of significance, the factors which are likely to influence the assurance achieved from a substantive test where the test involves sampling. These are six factors which reasoning suggests might affect the total assurance achieved from the sample whether or not formal statistical sampling plans are employed. After a discussion of these six factors there follows a discussion of the relevance of formal statistical sampling techniques to the problem of assessing assurance achieved from the sample.

The assurance *achieved* from any substantive test depends upon:

(1) *The method used to identify the representative sample.* The value of the results obtained from the representative component of the sample depends upon just how representative of the population it really is. For example, assume that the results obtained are consistent with the reported value of the population in the sense that no errors are found. The assurance provided by this depends in part upon how representative that sample is of the population. If it is unrepresentative, then little assurance may be attained. The auditor must try to have enough information about the accounting population under investigation to be able to select a representative sample. The risk of an unrepresentative sample increases significantly if certain sections of, or items in, the

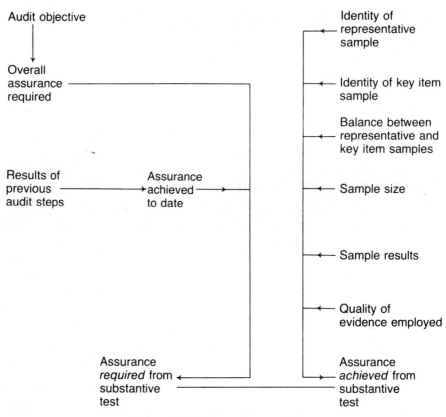

Figure 5.1   Substantive test design

population stand no chance of selection in the sample. Thus the auditor must guard against selecting items from incomplete listings of the transactions or balances in the accounting population. In addition, it is important to use a selection method, such as random sampling, which has a low risk of generating a significantly unrepresentative sample.

(2) *The method used to identify the sample of key items.* The auditor must have information, based on his previous audit steps, to be able to identify those items from which the 'key' item sample is selected. The better the quality of this information, the more the assurance achieved from the key item component of the sample.

(3) *Balance between representative and key item samples.* The existing balance between the representative and key item components of the overall sample affects the impact which any extension of either sample component has upon total assurance. If relatively very little attention has been paid to key items then a relatively large increase in assurance may be achieved by increasing the key item sample rather than the representative

sample. Similarly, if relatively little attention has been paid to the representative component then it may be desirable to increase the representative sample. The two components of the overall sample guard against different underlying error conditions in the population. If too little attention is paid to key items the sample may fail to discover the large but untypical errors. Too little attention to representative items would mean that the sample results may be unreasonably influenced by bias in the selection of sample items.

(4) *The number of items selected.* The auditor must come to a decision as to the size of the representative and key item samples. Other things being equal, the larger the sample the greater the assurance provided by the sample result.

(5) *The sample results actually obtained.* The number and type of errors actually discovered in the representative and key item samples determines, together with the other factors listed, the assurance achieved from the substantive testing. Other things being equal, the fewer the errors discovered in the sample the more assurance is obtained. The auditor cannot control the sample results, and it is through the manipulation of the other factors that the auditor obtains the assurance required.

(6) *The quality of evidence available to substantiate 'representative' and 'key' items.* For each item selected in the representative and key item samples, the auditor must select evidence to substantiate the transaction or balance with respect to the audit objective(s) of the test. It is possible to vary the quality of evidence obtained for different items selected in the sample and this possibility is discussed in Chapter 6 with reference to the audit of the validity of sales (pages 105 to 107).

The next section discusses the relevance of formal statistical sampling plans to an understanding of the relationship between the six factors identified as determining the assurance achieved from the substantive testing.

STATISTICAL SAMPLING AND SUBSTANTIVE TESTING

There are several statistical sampling techniques which are applied to auditing problems. Each technique specifies:

(1) A method for selecting the sample (*sample selection*); and
(2) A method for calculating a statistical report based on the results of the sample (*statistical evaluation*).

The first of these two processes is independent of the second, but not vice versa. In other words, it is possible to use the sample selection method specified by the technique but to evaluate the results judgmentally. It is not possible to use the sample evaluation specified by the technique unless the appropriate sample selection method has been used.

THE STATISTICAL EVALUATION

It is useful to consider separately the nature of the output of the evaluation
and the nature of the inputs to the evaluation. The statistical report is the
output of the statistical evaluation of the sample results. For nearly all
statistical sampling techniques of value to the auditor, it consists of the
following two elements:

(1) A range £$(R-Y)$ to £$(R+Z)$, where £R is the total value for the
population as reported in the financial statements. This range is sometimes known as the *confidence interval*.
(2) The risk ($X\%$) that the true total value of the population lies outside the
confidence interval.

The risk (X) is the risk that the true population lies in one of the shaded zones
of Figure 5.2 and hence is either understated by more than £Z *or* overstated
by more than £Y.

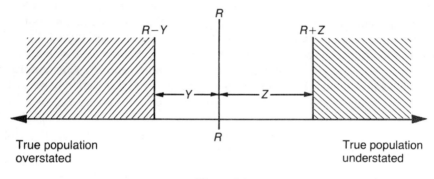

Figure 5.2

From the auditor's point of view the statistical report registers a higher
level of assurance in the reported population value

(1) The narrower the range about the reported population value, i.e. the
narrower the confidence interval; and
(2) The lower the risk associated with the confidence interval.

It is of little benefit having a low reported risk if the associated confidence
interval is too wide. Similarly, there is little benefit having a narrow reported
confidence interval if the associated risk is too high.

For most statistical sampling techniques, the *inputs* to the statistical
evaluation procedures are:

(1) The sample size and
(2) The rate and size of errors obtained.

Thus a statistical sampling technique of value to the auditor identifies the relationship between four factors:

Inputs: sample size, sample results
Outputs: confidence interval, risk.

It is the two inputs together with the relationship between inputs and outputs specified by the sampling technique (this relationship being different for different techniques) which determine the outputs, and hence the level of assurance in the reported population value indicated by the statistical report.

The relationship between the four factors provides that once three of the factors are given, the fourth factor can be determined. At the planning stage the relationship may be used by the auditor to suggest an appropriate sample

	Before the sample	After the sample	
	1	2	3
Sample size	Determined by statistics	Given	Given
Sample results	Expectation based on prior audit work	Given	Given
Confidence interval	Desired	Desired	Determined by statistics
Risk	Desired	Determined by statistics	Desired

Figure 5.3

size (Figure 5.3, column 1). The auditor specifies the *desired* value for confidence interval and risk and the *expected* rate and size of errors, and the statistics determine the necessary sample size. Once the sample is selected and the sample result obtained (Figure 5.3, column 2), then for any desired confidence interval the statistics determine the associated risk. (This risk will not equal the desired risk unless the sample result obtained matches expectation.)

Alternatively, once sample size and results are given for any desired risk (Figure 5.3, column 3), the statistics determine the associated confidence interval. Once again, this confidence interval will not equal the desired confidence interval unless the sample results match expectations. It follows that the relationship between the four factors, as specified by the statistical technique, allows the auditor to study the effect of a change in sample size or sample result or both upon the assurance achieved from the sample.

Suppose that for one sample size/sample result the following statement (statistical report) can be made on the basis of the statistical evaluation:

'There is a risk $X_1\%$ that the true population value lies outside the range $£(R-Y_1)$ to $£(R+Z_1)$, where R is the reported value',

and that, based on a second sample size/sample result from the same population, a second statement can be made:

'There is a risk $X_2\%$ that the true population value lies outside the range $£(R-Y_1)$ to $£(R+Z_1)$.'

If the stated confidence interval in the two statements is held constant at the desired level $((R-Y_1)$ to $(R+Z_1))$, then the movement in the risk (from X_1 to X_2) provides an indication of the change in achieved assurance consequent upon the change in the sample size and/or sample result. This can be extremely useful information for the auditor.

THE SAMPLE SELECTION

If the advantage of a statistical evaluation (i.e. an indication of assurance achieved) is desired, then it is necessary to select the sample on the basis specified by the chosen statistical technique. This basis will:

(a) Identify the representative sample (usually by means of some random selection technique);
(b) Identify the key item sample (if any – the less sophisticated techniques do not incorporate a key item component); and
(c) Determine the balance between the representative and key item components of the sample.

For example, two of the most useful statistical sampling techniques for audit purposes are stratified variables sampling (stratified estimation sampling for variables) and monetary unit sampling (referred to as dollar unit sampling in the United States and Canada). Stratified variables sampling requires the auditor to divide the population into strata according to the value of the items. The overall sample size is allocated to the various strata according to a predetermined formula, and random samples of the specified size are taken from each strata. Monetary unit sampling requires the auditor to regard a population of, say, debtors which totals £5 million as being a population of 5 million individual monetary units. Each of the 5 million monetary units is assigned a unique number between 1 and 5 million and a sample of monetary units is then selected at random from this total population. The result is a *representative* sample of monetary units which in turn means that large-value items in the population have a greater chance of representation in the sample than small-value items. This follows, since large-value items have a large number of monetary units in the population, and each monetary unit in the population has an equal chance of selection. In effect, there is an element of *key item* sampling of high-value items. In addition, the *balance* between the representative sample and the key item sample of high-value items is determined through the application of the sample selection technique, rather than being explicitly chosen by the auditor.

Statistical Evaluation and Assurance Achieved

In one important sense, once the sample has been selected and the sample results obtained, then the actual or real assurance achieved is determined. All that the statistical evaluation of the sample results does is to provide an indication or measure of this assurance achieved. However, if the assurance derived from the sample is assessed judgmentally without the benefit of the statistical measurement technique, prudence dictates that the auditor be cautious in his subjective measure of the assurance achieved. In another important sense, therefore, the uncertainty caused by the absence of the measuring technique and the need for prudence in these circumstances means that the assurance *which it is reasonable for the auditor to take* is less when a statistical evaluation technique is not in use than when it is in use. The effect of this can be to give the use of the measurement technique an appearance of providing assurance – but what it is really doing is reducing the need for prudence. The underlying real assurance is what is there waiting to be measured, and it provides an upper limit to the assurance which can be achieved, even assuming the most excellent measurement methods. This underlying real assurance is unaffected by the measurement methods employed.

Statistical evaluation attempts to provide an objective indication of the assurance which has actually been achieved. In a sense, the statistical evaluation does not change the underlying product (actual assurance achieved) but rather serves to advertise the product (i.e. bring to the auditor's attention the assurance achieved). Whether or not it advertises the product fairly depends upon the circumstances in which the technique is used, and this issue is discussed in the following paragraphs.

The risk (X) reported by the statistical technique deviates from the true risk

There are a variety of statistical sampling techniques available to the auditor, and the suitability of each technique depends upon the circumstances in which it is used. An empirical study of the performance of different statistical techniques found that no one technique is suited to all circumstances, but that in most circumstances there should be at least one technique which is suited. The authors of the study comment as follows: 'It is clear from this study that no one statistical procedure is optimal under all circumstances. However, the study has also shown that, for the populations and error patterns considered, there is no situation where at least one technique is not reasonably effective. Consequently, the auditor using statistical sampling must be familiar with a variety of statistical procedures and their comparative effectiveness so that he can choose an appropriate one for any particular circumstance.'[1]

If a statistical technique is used in circumstances to which it is unsuited, the risk reported by the technique can deviate significantly from the 'true' or actual risk which should be associated with the sample results. In the empirical study the 'true' or actual risk was approximated by repeating the application of the technique 600 times to a known accounting population. This involved the selection of 600 different samples of the same size and hence 600 sample results were obtained. For each sample result the desired level of risk (X_d) was held constant and the associated confidence interval was determined. Thus 600 confidence intervals were calculated and, since the risk was held constant, the confidence interval differed every time the sample result differed. The true or actual risk (X_a) associated with the use of the technique on the particular population was approximated by measuring the percentage of the 600 confidence intervals which failed to include the true population value (which was known to the experimenters). The level of risk (X_d) reported by the statistics was the same in each of the 600 applications. It is clear that if the reported risk (X_d) deviates significantly from the actual risk (X_a) then the technique is, for that particular population, likely to provide the auditor with misleading information. This is particularly danger-ous if the reported risk understates the actual risk.

The performance of the technique in different circumstances was investigated by changing the characteristics (including error rates and error patterns) of the population and repeating the 600 applications in each case. The experiments were repeated for a variety of statistical sampling techniques, and the experimenters found that techniques which performed well for some populations gave misleading results for others.

It follows that before any statistical sampling technique is used it is desirable for the auditor to have knowledge of:

(1) The characteristics of populations for which the technique may give misleading results; and
(2) Whether those characteristics are present in the population under audit.

Knowledge of the first kind is being made generally available to the auditing profession following the results of empirical studies such as the one described. Knowledge of the second kind is sometimes derived by the auditor as a result of earlier audit steps. For example,

(1) Population statistics provide knowledge of the 'shape' of the reported population, which, if there are few errors in the population, indicates the

'shape' of the population itself. The shape of the population is a factor affecting the performance of certain techniques.

(2) A study of internal control provides a basis for judging the likely error rate and the pattern of errors in the population. Once again, these are factors affecting the performance of certain techniques.

Before applying a statistical sampling technique it is desirable for the auditor to have knowledge of population characteristics. However, it should be recognised that the auditor can only have a limited knowledge of the population based on the earlier steps of the audit. If this were not the case, substantive testing would be unnecessary. The auditor may decide against the sampling technique which is optimal for the expected population characteristics if that technique is not sufficiently robust to give valid results should the population, in fact, be somewhat different from expectations.

Sample Selection and the Assurance Achieved

It is suggested in this chapter that the real assurance achieved from a sample is influenced by the sample selection procedures (method of identifying representative and key item samples, an appropriate balance between representative and key item sample sizes), rather than by the sample evaluation procedures. However, the selection method is specified by the chosen statistical sampling technique and it follows that the choice of sampling technique does affect the actual level of assurance achieved through the sample selection procedures. The fact that a selection method is compatible with a statistical sampling technique does not guarantee that it is an optimal method in the sense of achieving the highest real assurance for a given sample size. It does, however, mean that the statistical technique can be used to give an indication of the assurance achieved, provided that it is not used in circumstances where the technique gives misleading results.

Assurance Achieved and Assurance Required

Statistical sampling theory is capable of indicating, in certain circumstances, the level of assurance *achieved* from a given sample size and sample result. However, sampling theory cannot provide the answer as to how much assurance is *required* from the sample. The answer to this question must come from auditing, rather than statistical, theory. Unfortunately, audit evidence theory is essentially 'heuristic' rather than 'deterministic'. That is, the theory will indicate the direction in which the auditor should move, given a change in the circumstances, but not necessarily how far to move. For example, audit theory indicates that more assurance is required from the substantive testing (and hence sample sizes are larger) if the internal controls are weakened. However, if a particular internal control is removed from the system the theory does not give any precise answers as to how much more assurance is required or how much to increase sample size. The main thrust of audit evidence theory, therefore, is to achieve consistency between audits and between auditors rather than to establish absolute levels of performance. If the auditor does not extend substantive sample size when internal control weakens then, other things being equal, the auditor is being inconsistent. It is difficult to state categorically that a particular sample size is wrong except in the context of sample sizes used elsewhere in similar circumstances by the same or other auditors. Nevertheless, the constant probing of inconsistencies should, over a period of time, provide auditors with an understanding of sample size requirements.

Summary of Section on Statistical Sampling

Figure 5.4 provides a summary of the relationship between a statistical sampling technique and the factors listed in Figure 5.1 as influencing the quality of substantive testing. The reader should follow through Figure 5.4 in conjunction with the following notes, which are referred to on the face of the chart.

(1) The choice of statistical sampling technique determines the sample selection and sample evaluation procedures.

(2) The sample selection procedures in effect determine the way in which the representative and key item samples are selected, and the balance between the two.

(3) Sample size may be determined as that necessary for the statistical evaluation to give the desired confidence interval/risk on the basis of expected sample results.

(4) The method for identifying representative items, the method for identifying key items, the balance between the representative and key items, the sample size and sample results are five of the six factors determining the assurance actually achieved from the substantive testing (see Figure 5.1).

(5) The sample size and sample results are the two inputs to the statistical evaluation.

(6) The confidence interval and associated risk together form the output of the statistical evaluation, and may be used to provide an indication or measure of the assurance achieved from the sample.

(7) Any material divergence between the actual assurance achieved and the achievement indicated by the statistical evaluation should be traceable to one or more of the following:
  (a) Using a statistical technique in circumstances to which it is unsuited.
  (b) Non-sampling error.
  (c) The use of low-quality evidence to substantiate the sample items selected.

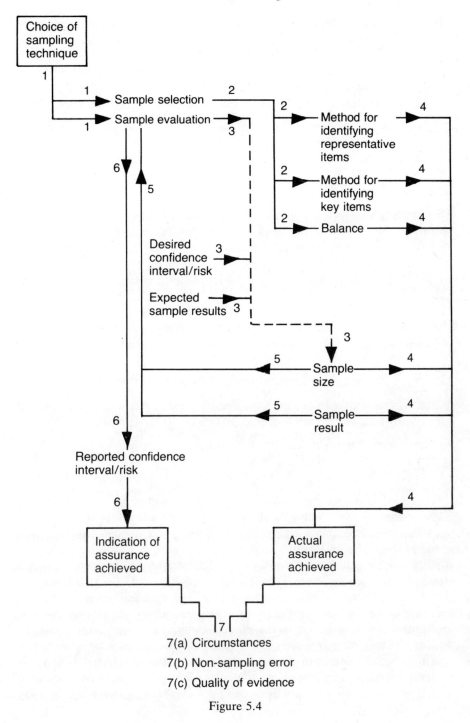

7(a) Circumstances

7(b) Non-sampling error

7(c) Quality of evidence

Figure 5.4

Non-sampling error

The use of sophisticated techniques by relatively untrained staff can cause:

(1) Computation errors in the calculation of risk (X) and confidence interval $£(R-Y)$ to $£(R+Z)$; and/or
(2) Misinterpretation of the meaning and significance of the statistical report.

Such errors are termed 'non-sampling', since they do not relate to the inadequacies of the statistical technique itself but to the failings of the people operating the technique or interpreting the statistical report.

The quality of evidence

One of the crucial factors determining the assurance achieved from substantive testing is the quality of the evidence used to substantiate the items in the sample. A statistical sampling technique cannot and does not provide any measure or indication of the quality of evidence used to substantiate sample items. Its indication of assurance achieved from the sample is based on the assumption that the evidence used is perfect and that the sample results, therefore, are accurate. It follows that when low-quality evidence is used to substantiate sample items, the assurance actually achieved may be considerably less than that indicated by the statistical evaluation.

Changes in evidence versus changes in sample size

When audit resources are scarce the auditor must decide whether a marginal unit of resource can increase overall assurance achieved more by:

(1) Improving the quality of evidence in support of existing sample items; or by
(2) Applying the evidence used to date to a larger number of sample items.

This issue is investigated further in the next chapter by reference to the audit of the validity of sales. In the first case, the quality of evidence used to substantiate sample items is improved but sample size remains constant. This is likely to be the preferred course of action when, to date, relatively poor quality evidence has been applied to a relatively large number of sample items. In these circumstances, an increase in the quality of evidence is likely to have a much more significant impact on total assurance than is a further increase in sample size. In the second case, the quality of evidence remains constant but sample size is increased. This might be the preferred course of action when, to date, relatively high-quality evidence has been applied to a relatively small number of sample items. In these circumstances, an increase in sample size may have a more significant impact on total assurance than would a further increase in the quality of evidence obtained for existing sample items.

A statistical technique cannot indicate changes in overall assurance achieved resulting from changes in the quality of evidence. It can only indicate changes in assurance achieved resulting from changes in sample size.

ASSESSING THE QUALITY OF EVIDENCE

When assessing the quality of evidence used in a substantive test the auditor should attempt to investigate the process which has created that evidence. In particular the auditor should examine:

(1) The relationship between the proposed substantive evidence and any underlying evidence from which the substantive evidence is derived; and
(2) The relationship between the underlying evidence and the economic event or condition requiring substantiation.

Substantive evidence may be created by the auditor, by the enterprise's accounting system, or by a third party.

Substantive Evidence Created by the Accounting System

Where the evidence has been processed or generated by the enterprise's accounting system, that system must be studied by the auditor in order to assess the quality of the substantive evidence. For example, to assess the quality of a sales invoice as evidence of a despatch it is necessary to examine:

(1) The relationship between the sales invoice (proposed substantive evidence) and the despatch note (underlying evidence) from which the sales invoice is prepared by the enterprise's staff. A study of this relationship involves a study of the accounting system; and
(2) The relationship between the despatch note (underlying evidence) and the despatch of goods (economic event requiring substantiation). This involves a study of the circumstances in which the despatch note is created.

To examine the quality of a despatch note (as opposed to a sales invoice) as substantive evidence of despatch it is only necessary to examine the second of these relationships.

It is likely that both the relationships will already have been examined during the auditor's investigation of the accounting system and its internal controls, and that assurance in the financial statements will have been taken from that investigation. The degree of independence of the substantive evidence from the accounting system and its internal controls is a factor influencing the marginal assurance obtained from the substantive testing once the internal controls have been investigated. Ideally, the substantive evidence should be independent of internal control, and should, therefore, be capable of substantiating a transaction irrespective of the condition of internal control. This ideal is not possible when the substantive evidence is created by the accounting system. The quality of a sales invoice as evidence of despatch is dependent upon two relationships determined by the accounting system. The quality of a despatch note as evidence of despatch depends upon one relationship determined by the accounting system. Although the despatch note has greater independence than the sales invoice it is still dependent for its creation upon one operation within the accounting system.

Substantive Evidence Created by a Third Party

The process used by the third party to create the substantive evidence, together with the ability and motive of the third party, determines the quality of third party evidence.

Processes used

The most important consideration is likely to be the relationship between

(1) The underlying evidence used by the third party in the process of substantive evidence creation; *and*
(2) The economic event or condition requiring substantiation.

Consider two different examples of third party evidence:

A = certificate from bank giving bank balance at a specified date.
B = a report from a surveyor giving a property valuation at a specified date.

Suppose that, to provide evidence A, the bank examines the particular bank account, and that controls over the bank accounts are good. If controls are good, a study of the bank account should be capable of exactly determining the bank balance. In the case of evidence A, the underlying evidence (the bank account and its controls) has a strong relationship (it should be an exact relationship) with the matter requiring substantiation (the bank balance). Suppose that, to provide evidence B, the surveyor examines the recent sale price of similar properties in similar locations. It is not possible to determine exactly the market value of a particular property on this basis. In the case of evidence B, the underlying evidence (sales of similar properties) does not have such a strong relationship with the matter requiring substantiation (the value of the particular property).

Judgmental interpretation of the underlying evidence by the surveyor is necessary before the property valuation can be given. It follows that evidence such as B, whilst it may be the best available, is judgmental and, other things being equal, not of the same quality as evidence such as A, where the underlying supportive evidence does not require judgmental interpretation by the third party.

This discussion on the underlying processes used to create third party evidence has focused on the quality of evidence provided by, and hence assurance achieved from, the bank certificate and surveyor's report. The assurance achieved from the bank certificate is likely to exceed that achieved from the surveyor's report. However, it is quite possible that the assurance required, in terms of financial statement user expectations, is higher for the bank figure than it is for the property valuation. The user is aware that the bank figure should be capable of exact verification but that the property valuation is not, and builds this awareness into his expectations. In these circumstances, it is quite possible for the assurance requirements for both the bank figure and the property valuation to be satisfied but with evidence of differing quality.

Ability and motive

The quality of third party evidence is influenced by the ability and motive of the third party. Ability must be judged in the context of the task to be performed. For example, the level of skill necessary to produce the balance for the bank certificate is less than that required for the property valuation. In addition, the skills are different and the skill possessed by the third party must be relevant to the third party evidence. Where a high level of skill is required it may be appropriate for the auditor to take into consideration the qualifications and previous experience of the third party. The auditor can also take into account his own experience of past dealings with the third party, and whether similar third party evidence has proved reliable in the past.

Motive may be influenced by the third party's independence (or lack of independence) from the enterprise undergoing audit. If the third party is appointed by the auditor rather than by the enterprise, then the independence of the third party from the enterprise is likely to be greater. For example, it is possible for the auditor, with the permission of enterprise management, to commission an independent valuation of property. Whether or not the third party is appointed by the auditor, it is highly desirable that the evidence should be passed direct from the third party to the auditor, and not travel via the enterprise, with the obvious possible risk of interference by enterprise management.

Further considerations might be whether the third party is a member of a professional body and/or the consequences to the third party if incorrect evidence is given. If the third party is a member of a professional body it is to be hoped that the level of motivation might be higher than in other circumstances! If the consequences of incorrect evidence to the third party are serious, then it might be expected that a higher level of motivation would be present. For example, a debtor would not be expected to confirm a significantly overstated debt. A bank would not be expected to report an incorrect bank balance, since to do so might damage the bank's reputation. However, the auditor should also pay attention to his past experience of third party evidence, and experience shows that debtors do sometimes confirm overstated debts, and that banks, on occasion, report incorrect balances.

Problems in Assessing Third Party Evidence

Two distinct problems limit the auditor's ability to assess the quality of third party evidence:

(1) The auditor's inability to obtain knowledge of the process used to create third party evidence.
(2) The auditor's inability to understand the process used to create third party evidence.

It should be remembered that where an auditor is unable, or does not choose, to assess the process which has created the third party evidence, then the quality of the evidence is unchanged but the auditor's ability to assess the quality of the evidence is significantly reduced.

Inability to obtain knowledge

The third party may be unwilling to disclose the process by which the third party evidence is created. Knowledge of third party processes may, however, sometimes be obtained by one of the following means:

(1) Professional guidance notes: for example, the Royal Institute of Chartered Surveyors issue guidance notes on how their members should value a property for financial statement purposes.
(2) Instructions to the third party; the third party may be given detailed written instructions by either the enterprise's management or the auditor as to what should be done before the third party evidence is prepared.
(3) A long form report: generally third party evidence takes the form of a brief written statement or certificate. It may, however, if requested by the enterprise management or the auditor, occasionally take the form of a detailed report of work done and underlying evidence used.
(4) Questionnaire: the auditor may request the third party to complete a questionnaire relating to the work done and underlying evidence used. In addition, the auditor may request an interview with the third party. A questionnaire is used, for example, by the group auditors (where the group and subsidiary auditors are different) to obtain information from the auditors of subsidiary companies as to the work done and underlying evidence used in the subsidiary's audit.

Inability to understand

Where the auditor does have access to the process used by the third party, there are a number of ways in which the auditor can proceed:

(1) The auditor can still choose to rely on the evidence of the third party without any examination of the process used to create the evidence. In this case the auditor relies entirely upon the abilities of the third party.
(2) The auditor scans both the underlying evidence and reasoning upon which the third party evidence is based. The auditor is more concerned to see that the underlying evidence and reasoning exist rather than to examine either in any detail. He relies upon the third party to have got the reasoning right, but is satisfied that the reasoning has taken place.
(3) The auditor follows through the reasoning of the third party (possibly under the guidance of the third party), and then assesses the suitability of the reasoning and underlying evidence upon which the third party's conclusion is based.
(4) The auditor independently interprets the underlying evidence without reference to the reasoning of the third party and then compares his conclusion with the conclusion of the third party and examines any difference.
(5) The auditor independently interprets the underlying evidence without reference to the reasoning of the third party and ignores the conclusion of the third party.

There is, therefore, a spectrum of involvement for the auditor with the third party evidence. This spectrum goes from the auditor taking the third party evidence without enquiry (position (1)) through to the auditor completely ignoring the reasoning of the third party, and using the third party merely as a source of underlying evidence (position (5)). Various intermediate positions on the spectrum are identified and in practice there are no doubt other intermediate positions which are taken by auditors in relation to third party evidence.

It should be clear that those positions such as (4) and (5) in which there is a high degree of involvement on the part of the auditor are only feasible if the auditor is highly competent to interpret the underlying evidence. They are rarely practical when the underlying evidence requires specialist interpretation. In this case, it may be practical for the auditor to follow through the work of a specialist, but it is unlikely that the auditor can perform an independent interpretation of the evidence without help. For example, it may be possible for the auditor to follow through and question the reasoning of an actuary in the computation of an actuarial surplus (position (3)). It would not generally be possible for an auditor to compute the actuarial surplus without reference to the actuary's work, even if the auditor had access to the underlying information upon which the computations were based.

There are many examples of the auditor obtaining evidence from third parties who have expertise different from the auditor:

Property valuers
Actuaries
Bankers
Lawyers
Government officers
Engineers
Architects
Assayers

The auditor cannot necessarily be expected to match these specialist skills but he might be expected to probe the work done by the specialist. One of the tasks of the professional accountancy bodies is to explain to other professional groups the nature of the audit evidence problem with respect to evidence from specialists, and to promote an understanding on the part of other professional groups that it may be appropriate for the auditor to examine their methods.

Clearly, the ability of the auditor to understand the work done by specialist third parties is a limiting factor on the ability of the auditor to assess the quality of such third party evidence. Where the specialist third party evidence is fundamental to the audit, it may be desirable for the auditor to develop specialist knowledge at least to the extent necessary to be able to follow and intelligently question the work performed by the specialist (position (3)). However, where the third party evidence is of much less importance to the audit, it may be reasonable for the auditor to rely on the evidence of a suitably qualified specialist without examining the specialist's work in detail (positions (1) or (2)).

EFFECTIVE SUBSTANTIVE TESTING

This chapter has introduced an important distinction between the underlying assurance actually achieved by the substantive testing and the auditor's ability to recognise or measure the underlying assurance achieved. Of course, if the auditor is unable to measure the underlying assurance achieved it does not preclude him taking some assurance from the substantive test results. However, the uncertainty about the assurance actually achieved should cause the auditor to be cautious, and to take less assurance from the test results than is actually achieved. Alternatively, the auditor may not be cautious, and may take more assurance than is actually achieved. Clearly, this is dangerous, and it is to be hoped that most auditors err on the side of caution. Improvements in the auditor's ability to measure assurance reduce the need for caution, and allow the assurance taken by the auditor to approach the assurance actually achieved.

It was suggested (Figure 5.1) that the assurance actually achieved depends upon six factors:

(1) Quality of identification of representative sample items.
(2) Quality of identification of key items.
(3) The balance between the representative and key item samples.
(4) Sample size.
(5) Sample results.
(6) Quality of evidence used to substantiate sample items.

In relation to the first five factors, the ability of the auditor to recognise the assurance achieved depends upon the suitability of any statistical technique used for evaluation purposes. In relation to the sixth factor (quality of evidence), the ability of the auditor to recognise the assurance achieved depends upon the auditor's ability to assess and interpret the process by which the evidence is created.

Given the scarcity of audit resources, the auditor must make the decision whether to invest a marginal unit of audit time in pursuit of:

(a) An increase in actual assurance achieved; *or*
(b) An increase in the auditor's ability to measure or recognise the actual assurance achieved.

A proper balance between these two objectives is crucial to effective substantive testing. The first objective may be attained through

(1) An improved selection method for representative and key item samples.
(2) An increased sample size and a better balance between the representative and key item samples.
(3) An increased selection of evidence to substantiate sample items.

The second objective may be attained through:

(1) An improved statistical evaluation technique.
(2) A more thorough investigation of the processes by which the evidence used to substantiate sample items is created.

It should be remembered that the substantive testing need be no more effective than is necessary to provide the assurance required after considering the assurance obtained from earlier steps of the audit process.

REFERENCE

1. Neter, J., and Loebbecke, J. K., *Behaviour of Major Statistical Estimators in Sampling Accounting Populations. An Empirical Study* (A.I.C.P.A. Auditing Research Monograph 2, 1975), p. 139.

6 Sales and Debtors

This chapter discusses the quality of evidence typically used in the design of substantive tests for sales as well as with the problems of identifying populations and key items for the sales audit tests. The discussion of sales proceeds on an objective-by-objective basis. The chapter then continues with a discussion of the substantive tests for debtors, and focuses on the debtors circularisation as being the primary source of evidence used by auditors in the substantiation of debtors.

SUBSTANTIVE TESTS FOR SALES: THE VALIDITY OBJECTIVE

Before embarking on the audit of the validity of sales it is imperative that the auditor studies, as part of the acquisition of knowledge of the business, the terms and conditions of sale which the business operates. These terms dictate the criteria against which the validity of a sale should be judged. Typically, the validity of a sale may be judged by whether there has been a despatch of serviceable goods to a customer's order. However, in some businesses the criteria will be different. For example, any one of the following *may* provide complications:

(1) Conditions of sale include a reservation of title by the seller until payment is received.
(2) Stock despatched on 'consignment' under 'sale or return' arrangements.
(3) Long-term contracts.
(4) Hire purchase sales.

However, in the discussion which follows it is assumed that the conditions of sale do not introduce any such complications.

Planning the 'Validity' Tests

Figure 6.1 is in the form of a working paper which might be used for the substantive tests of the validity of sales.

The validity of sales is generally an audit objective which requires a high overall level of assurance from all audit tests (line 1). In Figure 6.1 it is *assumed for illustrative purposes* that a low level of assurance has been achieved from previous audit steps (line 2) and this leaves a high level of assurance still to be obtained from the substantive testing (line 3). Lines 4 to 7 specify the details of the substantive test. No attempt is made in this illustration to specify sample size (line 4). As indicated in previous discussion on sample sizes, the choice of sample size is, although assisted by statistical

Sales Audit: Validity	
(1) Overall assurance required	High
(2) Assurance achieved to date	Low
(3) Assurance required	High
(4) Sample size: Representative Key item	x (Random) y
(5) Population for representative sample	Sales day book entries
(6) Evidence employed	(1) Order (2) Despatch (3) Copy invoice (4) Cash receipt
(7) Key items	(1) Out-of-sequence copy invoices (2) Copy invoices unmatched with despatch (3) Long-overdue sales
(8) Substantive test results	
(9) Assurance achieved	

Figure 6.1   Substantive test planning schedule

theory, an heuristic decision. Different auditing firms have developed different procedures for determining sample size. These procedures are somewhat arbitrary, although they do have the merit of promoting consistency within each of the auditing firms concerned. Line 4 shows that the representative sample is selected at random.

Line 5 identifies the population used for the selection of representative items. In this case, the population of entries in the sales day book is used. The auditor guards against incompleteness of this population by ensuring that the sales day book totals to the sales figure in the financial statements. This constitutes a separate substantive test relevant to the summation objective.

Line 6 specifies the evidence employed in the test to substantiate the items selected in the representative sample. A valid sale should have been:

(1) The subject of a customer's order;
(2) Despatched;
(3) Invoiced;
(4) The cause of a cash receipt.

If the auditor is unable to achieve the required assurance on the basis of this evidence, it is possible to obtain direct confirmation of the sale from the customer.

Line 7 specifies the sources used to identify key items. In this case, the auditor concentrates on out-of-sequence copy invoices, copy invoices unmatched with despatches, and sales for which the cash receipt is long overdue. To discover these key items the auditor scans the file of copy invoices (assuming that they have been filed sequentially), ascertains the location of unmatched copy invoices, and scans the sales ledger for long-overdue items. It is not generally necessary to substantiate every such key item: a sample of key items should be taken. In order to substantiate key items, reference is made to the same documentary evidence as for the representative items (minus any missing documents) *and* an explanation is sought as to why the invoice is out of sequence, unmatched or unpaid, as the case may be.

The assurance achieved from the substantive test (line 9) depends upon the factors listed in lines 4 to 7 together with the number and type of errors actually discovered. The substantive test results are recorded on line 8. In planning lines 4 to 7, the auditor, of course, does not know the test results. These must be anticipated, using the planning information derived from earlier audit steps, so that if the expected results are realised, the assurance achieved equals the assurance required. If the results are worse than expected, assurance achieved is less than required, and the auditor must perform further audit work to bridge the gap. The nature of this further work is discussed later in this chapter (pages 113–116).

Substantive and Compliance Tests

At this point it is once again instructive to consider the distinction between substantive and compliance tests. Enterprise management may, as part of the internal control procedures, have investigated out-of-sequence, unmatched or unpaid invoices. If the auditor wishes to perform a compliance test of such control procedures it is only necessary for the auditor to *scan* evidence, preferably in the form of written reports demonstrating that management has performed its investigation and established the position as satisfactory. It is not necessary, for compliance test purposes, for the auditor to effectively re-perform the enterprise's investigation by *studying in detail* and validating the findings of the investigation. Such a re-performance, albeit assisted by the enterprise's working papers, is necessary for the substantive test in which the auditor must attempt to validate the findings of the enterprise and the explanations given by the enterprise. In a compliance test the enterprise's working papers are used as evidence of performance by the enterprise's management. In a substantive test the performance is by the auditor, and the enterprise's working papers are used to expedite the auditor's own investigation.

Once again this demonstrates the fact that compliance and substantive tests may utilise the same evidence, but that the degree of involvement of the auditor with the evidence is different in the two cases. In compliance testing the auditor typically 'scans' the evidence, and the choice of the word 'scan' implies a low degree of involvement in detail. In substantive testing, however, the auditor typically studies the evidence in much greater detail.

QUALITY OF EVIDENCE AND SAMPLE SIZE

Figure 6.1 indicates that four pieces of evidence (order, despatch, copy invoice, cash receipt) are available for the substantiation of individual items selected in the representative sample. However, it is not necessarily desirable that the auditor should use all four pieces of evidence in support of each sample item.

If there were, say, 100 items in the substantive sample and there are four pieces of evidence available to support each sample item, there is a total of 400 pieces of evidence available from the sample to support the validity of sales. This would be a typical situation in practice. However, the principles underlying the selection of evidence from the 400 pieces can be demonstrated using the simplest possible illustration of two items (S1, S2) in the sample and two available pieces of evidence (e1, e2) for each item, giving a total of four available pieces of evidence (A, B, C, D) as shown in Figure 6.2.

Consider the following possible combinations of pieces of evidence: AB, AC, ABC, and ABCD. The assurance derived from ABCD will exceed the assurance derived from ABC, which in turn will exceed that derived from either AB or AC. The assurance from AB may or may not exceed the assurance from AC depending on whether it is better to have more evidence (e1 and e2) in support of fewer sample items (S1), or less evidence (e1) in

	e1	e2
S1	A	B
S2	C	D

Figure 6.2

support of a larger number of sample items (S1 and S2). This will vary depending upon the circumstances, but suppose, for illustrative purposes, the assurance levels *achieved* from the four combinations of evidence are as shown in Figure 6.3. The selected combination of evidence then depends upon the *required* level of assurance as shown in Figure 6.4.

Level 1

If the required assurance is at level 1, the auditor will select the less expensive option of AB and AC. If AB is selected, the implication is that the sample size should be smaller than specified, since only one (S1) of the two items is studied. If AC is selected, the implication is that not all the available evidence is required, since only one (e1) of the two types of evidence is studied.

Level 2

If the required assurance is at level 2, the auditor will select combination AC, this being less expensive than ABC or ABCD.

Level 3

If the required assurance is at level 3, the auditor will select combination ABC as being less expensive than ABCD. The implication of this selection is that the quality of evidence obtained for some sample items is higher than for others. In this case, both types of available evidence (e1 and e2) are employed for the first sample item (S1), and only one (e1) for the second sample item (S2).

Level 4

If the required assurance is at level 4, the auditor will select combination ABCD. If the required assurance is at any higher level, the implication is that the existing sample size is too small.

If the outcome of this selection process is either combination AC or ABC, then the auditor is not using all the available evidence for each sample item. If the auditor has 100 sample items and the four pieces of evidence (order, despatch, copy invoice and cash receipt) are available for each item, then a possible evidence selection would be, for example,

(1) Order, despatch, copy invoice and cash receipt – first 20 items.
(2) Despatch, copy invoice and cash receipt – further 30 items.
(3) Despatch, cash receipt – further 30 items.
(4) Despatch only – final 20 items.

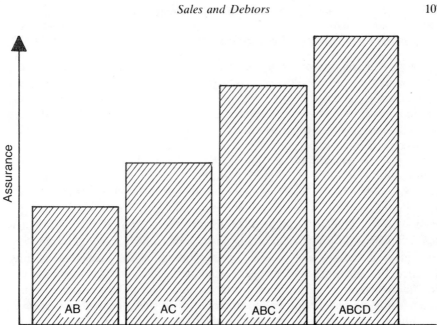

Figure 6.3   Assurance achieved

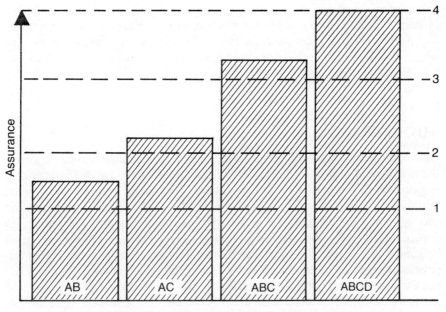

Figure 6.4   Assurance achieved and required

Assessing the quality of evidence

To assess the quality of a piece of evidence the auditor asks the question as to how likely is an invalid sale given the existence of the piece of evidence. For example, given that the customer has paid, an invalid sale is unlikely. Hence a cash receipt is strong evidence of a valid sale provided that the cash receipt is clearly identified as coming from the customer concerned and as relating to the sale concerned. For the auditor the problem of identifying cash receipts with sales may, in many cases, make the cash receipt a time-consuming source of evidence. Identifying despatches, orders and copy invoices with sales is generally much easier, but the quality of this evidence, being generated by the accounting system under the enterprise's control, is more suspect. Hence the auditor is forced to trade-off high-quality, high-cost (in terms of audit time) evidence against comparatively low-quality, low-cost evidence. Although always open to the possibility of management interference, documentary evidence generated by the accounting system does vary in quality according to the quality of the system. The auditor must understand the accounting system and its internal controls if such documentary evidence is to be properly assessed. A good system should ensure that every order is despatched and that every despatch is invoiced. In a good system, therefore, having established one of the three pieces of evidence, the other two pieces of evidence are expected, and it follows that with a good system there is little independence between the order, despatch and copy invoice. The auditor will be inclined to study just one (probably the despatch) rather than all three documents, since the marginal assurance derived from 'non-independent' evidence is small. This is a further illustration of how a good system reduces the need to rely upon detailed substantive tests. It is not only the sample size which may be reduced, but also the number of pieces of evidence which it is felt necessary to consult in order to substantiate each item.

AUTHORISATION

Before designing the substantive tests relevant to the authorisation objective the auditor must decide what constitutes an 'authorised' sale. An enterprise is entitled to develop its own authorisation procedures, and one view of an 'authorised' transaction is simply one which has undergone the authorisation procedures of the enterprise. Following this view, the auditor's responsibility regarding authorisation is primarily one of compliance, and there is only a relatively minor role for substantive tests. For example, suppose the enterprise's procedures require sales to be authorised by a responsible official and the official evidences the authorisation by signing the order. In this case, the main thrust of the authorisation audit is to compliance test the operation of the control by reference to an observation of the signature on the sales orders.

The substantive testing may be restricted to an investigation of those sales which, as evidenced by the absence of a signature, have missed the control procedure. This would be a key item sample.

An alternative view of the 'authorised' sale is that it is not merely a sale which has undergone the enterprise's authorisation procedures but a sale which it was reasonable, in the circumstances prevailing at the time, for the enterprise to make. Following this view, the key item sample is likely to be extended to include a selection of high-value sales to high-risk customers in terms of credit rating. The auditor would ascertain from the official concerned the reasons for having given authorisation in these instances. Of course, in practice, if not in theory, it is difficult for the auditor to judge that a sale should not have been made if subsequently payment has been received. There is, therefore, a tendency to concentrate attention on the authorisation of unpaid sales, in which case the authorisation of transactions audit merges with the audit of the recoverability of debtors.

COMPLETENESS

Figure 6.5 is an excerpt from a substantive test planning schedule which illustrates substantive tests relevant to the completeness objective. Basically, the auditor wishes to take a representative sample of issued orders and a sample of issued despatches and to check that they have resulted in a sales invoice, which is subsequently entered in the sales day book. In designing any substantive test it is important that the population from which the sample is selected is complete. When the objective of the test is completeness, this factor clearly becomes crucial. The auditor is concerned on two counts:

(1) That the listing or file of documents from which the sample is selected contains all the documents issued (sales orders and despatch notes),
(2) That a document is issued to record each and every underlying economic event (i.e. actual orders and despatches).

Consider the second of these concerns. It is difficult to devise any substantive tests for completeness unless the conditions in which sales orders

Population for representative sample	(1) Issued sales order numbers (2) Issued despatch numbers
Evidence employed	(1) Copy sales invoice (2) Sales day book entry
Key items	(1) Unmatched despatches (2) Unmatched cash receipts

Figure 6.5   The completeness objective

and despatch notes are issued suggest that these documents themselves form a complete record of events. *The auditor must study the operation in the accounting system which creates these source documents.* Without sound source documents no substantive testing is possible.

Consider the first of these concerns. A test can be devised to ensure that the listing or file of documents is complete, provided that the documents are pre-numbered and issued in sequence. This can be done as follows:

(1) Select a block of numbers within the range of issued numbers; and/or
(2) Select a random sample of numbers within the range of issued numbers,

and for each selected number check the presence in the listing or file of the numbered document. The random sample of numbers has the advantage that it can be used as the representative sample for checking to the copy sales invoice and sales day book entry. The block of numbers has the advantage that a sequence check can, provided the listing or file is in numerical order, be performed speedily. It might be used as a supplement to the random sample of numbers. However, in the illustration given in Figure 6.5, the sequence check is not used.

The key item sample suggested in this figure concentrates on despatches which may not have been invoiced (unmatched despatches) and cash receipts which the enterprise is unable to identify with any recorded invoice (unmatched cash). This could happen, for example, if the sales invoice is sent to the customer but is not recorded in the ledgers.

CUT-OFF

A cut-off test for *completeness* has as its objective to ensure that despatches issued shortly before the end of the accounting period are included in sales for the period. The auditor should note the number of the last despatch and select a sample of despatches with numbers close to, but slightly less than, that terminal number. The auditor checks that the selected despatches were included in sales for the period. Such a cut-off test is itself, in effect, a key item sample relevant to the completeness objective, since sales close to the period-end have a greater than average chance of being improperly omitted from the period's sales.

A cut-off test for *validity* has as its objectives to ensure that sales included in the sales day book shortly before the end of the accounting period were despatched before the end of the period *and* were wanted by the customer. To satisfy the first of these objectives, the auditor.should select a sample of the last entries in the sales day book for the accounting period and check that they were despatched before the period-end. To satisfy the second objective, the auditor checks that the sales were ordered by the customer and have neither been returned nor otherwise given credit for, in the new accounting period. Such a cut-off test is itself, in effect, a key item sample relevant to the validity objective.

VALUATION

Figure 6.6 is an excerpt from a substantive test planning schedule for the valuation objective illustrating the type of tests which are relevant. There are three basic stages in the valuation audit:

(1) Checking the quantities;
(2) Checking the prices;
(3) Checking the price times quantity multiples and invoice additions.

It is assumed in Figure 6.6 that quantities have been already checked to despatch notes and orders as part of the validity audit. It remains for the auditor to check the computations of a sample of invoices and to check the

Population for representative sample	Copy invoices
Evidence employed	(1) Recomputation (2) Prices to standing data (3) Standing data prices to authorised amendments
Key items	(1) Invoices unchecked by client (2) Debit notes referring to valuation errors

Figure 6.6   The valuation objective

prices. Prices should be checked to a standard data listing of selling prices and, for a percentage of the sales selected in the sample, the prices per the standing data might be checked to the latest authorised amendment.

There are two views as to the significance of the valuation objective. One view is that once the invoice is accepted and paid by the customer the value per the sales invoice is the value of the sale, irrespective of whether the price actually charged was properly authorised and the invoice value properly calculated. The idea is that once a transaction has been completed to the satisfaction of both buyer and seller, it is unlikely that any further investigation of the valuation of the transaction will take place, and in reality the invoice value becomes the value of the sale. Following this view, the valuation objective is given little prominence, and the auditor concentrates upon an assessment of value for the unpaid and disputed invoices. The valuation of transactions audit merges with the audit of the valuation of debtors. The accounting effect of this view is that any losses occasioned by incorrect invoicing are reflected in a lower profit figure but are not separately disclosed.

A second view is that the value of a sale is the value at which it should have been invoiced, assuming that the price is properly authorised and the invoice value properly calculated. Any material losses occasioned by incorrect invoicing should, by implication, be separately disclosed. Following this view, the valuation objective is given much greater prominence by the auditor, and the required assurance level set accordingly.

CLASSIFICATION

In the audit of purchases it is vital to check the classification of the purchases into period or product costs (i.e. expense or stock items). In the audit of sales there is no similar classification requirement which, if not met, would affect profit.

The possible inclusion in sales of items not properly classified as sales is examined as part of the validity audit. If, however, the financial statements disclose a breakdown of sales into different categories the auditor should check a sample of sales as to whether they have been included in the appropriate category.

SUMMATION

There are three stages in the summation process:

(1) Sales invoices are listed in the sales day book;
(2) The sales day book is cast;
(3) The total per the sales day book is transferred to the ledger account for sales.

The auditor must check each stage. In the audit of the first stage a sample of copy sales invoices may be checked to the sales day book. In the audit of the second stage the casts of the sales day book may be re-performed by the auditor. In the audit of the third stage the totals per the sales day book may be traced to the ledger account for sales and hence to the sales figure in the financial statements.

Delay between the performance of audit tests is the Achilles heel of the auditor. The auditor must ensure that the sales day book (both totals and details) remains unaltered during the period over which the audit tests – especially those relating to the summation, validity and valuation objectives – are conducted.

DISCLOSURE

The auditor must be satisfied that the level of disclosure, including the extent to which sales is broken down into different categories, is consistent with the true and fair view and/or other requirements.

FURTHER AUDIT WORK

In planning the details of the substantive tests, the auditor must anticipate the test results on the basis of the prior knowledge acquired in earlier steps of the audit process. The auditor plans the substantive testing on the expectation that the test results will prove consistent with the other steps of the audit process. If they turn out to be inconsistent because the actual results are worse than expected, then the assurance achieved falls short of expectations and of the assurance required. Since substantive testing is relatively high-quality audit evidence it is likely that the auditor will try to bridge the gap by further substantive testing. This may take one or more of the following forms:

(1) A detailed study of the reasons for the errors discovered in the initial sample;
(2) A further key item sample using information derived from a study of the errors obtained in the initial sample;
(3) A further representative sample selected from the same population as the initial sample.

Study of the 'Errors' Discovered in the Initial Sample

It is useful to consider what is meant by the term 'error' when used in this connection. Two possible situations should be distinguished:

(1) The evidence studied in the substantive test *indicates* that there *may be* an error in the transaction (i.e. the transaction may be invalid or un-authorised, etc.) but does not confirm the existence of the error;
(2) The evidence studied provides *convincing* evidence of the existence of an error.

The word 'indicates' means that while the auditor has useful evidence to support the proposition that a transaction is in error; there is not *sufficient* evidence to support the proposition. The word 'convincing' means that there is sufficient evidence to support the proposition.

In the majority of cases the 'errors' discovered in the substantive testing reflect the first situation rather than the second. By way of illustration, consider the substantive test for the validity of sales. A sales order, despatch, copy invoice and cash receipt together are considered to provide convincing evidence of the validity of a sale. However, whenever evidence is missing or is inconsistent with the validity of a transaction it is not necessarily convincing evidence that the transaction is invalid. The absence of a despatch note and cash receipt is indicative of the possibility of an invalid sale, but further enquiries (possibly including contact with the customer concerned) would have to be made to provide convincing evidence of invalidity. The despatch note could simply be mislaid, and the invoice as yet unpaid by the customer.

Whenever the evidence studied in the substantive test indicates that there may be error in the transaction, further evidence must be studied to ascertain whether or not the error actually exists. Such evidence generally includes enquiries into how there came to be the missing or inconsistent evidence discovered in the test.

There are three possible outcomes of the study of such errors discovered in the initial sample:

Outcome 1

Transactions indicated by the initial sample to be in error are found on the basis of further evidence to be correct.

Outcome 2

The reasons for the error may indicate to the auditor a category of key items unrecognised by the initial sample. For example, the errors may be limited to a particular time period, a particular type of transaction or a particular location or department. If so, sample size is increased within the defined limits rather than generally. A further key item sample is taken using information derived from a study of the errors obtained in the initial sample.

Outcome 3

The errors do not appear limited to any particular category of transactions, and the representative sample is extended. A further representative sample is taken from the same population as the initial sample.

In the case of outcomes 2 or 3, as the auditor extends the sample two significant points are reached:

(1) As soon as the sample and the number of errors found are large enough to give a good indication that there is material error in the population, the auditor should approach the enterprise's staff to see if they are willing to mount their own investigation.
(2) If the enterprise is unwilling to mount its own investigation the sample is extended further until the sample results either provide convincing evidence that the error is immaterial or convincing evidence that the error is material. In the latter case, sample results can either be used as

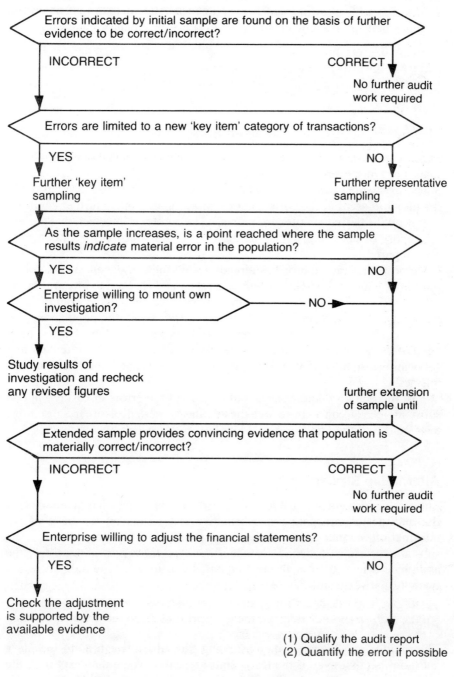

Figure 6.7   Programme of further audit work when achieved
assurance falls short of required assurance

the basis of an adjustment to the financial statements or, if enterprise management are unwilling to adjust, to justify a qualified audit report.

Figure 6.7 sets out in the form of a decision chart the programme of further audit work which the auditor should perform when the achieved assurance from the substantive test falls short of that required.

The Interrelationships between Substantive Tests

Suppose the auditor is testing the validity of sales. A sample of entries in the sales day book is taken and checked, amongst other things, to the despatch notes. In several cases the despatch note is absent. Following the discussion in the previous section, the correct course of action is to make further enquiries as to why the despatch notes are missing. The auditor is informed that there is a category of sales (e.g. repairs and servicing) for which despatch notes are not prepared.

Suppose that the auditor has already tested the completeness of sales. A sample of issued despatch numbers was taken and checked to an entry in the sales day book. Through enquiries into errors discovered in the validity audit, the auditor has obtained information which shows that the population used for the completeness substantive test is itself incomplete. A further test must be devised to examine the completeness of sales invoices for repairs and servicing (assuming that this represents a significant component of the business).

This illustration demonstrates that a study of the errors discovered in one substantive test can expose weaknesses in the design of other substantive tests, and that the auditor should be alert to this possibility.

Alternative Strategies

The strategy for substantive test design which this chapter has adopted is for the auditor to anticipate the substantive test results on the basis of the information contained in the earlier steps of the audit process. The substantive test is designed so that *if the expected results are realised*, the assurance achieved from the test equals the assurance required. There are two alternatives to this strategy:

Alternative 1

The auditor may decide, when planning the substantive test, to include a 'cushion', so that even if the test results are rather worse than expected, the achieved assurance can still match the assurance required. However, this alternative has the inefficiency caused by achieved assurance exceeding required assurance whenever expectations are realised in the sample results or the sample results are better than expected.

Alternative 2

The auditor may plan the substantive test so that, even if the test results are consistent with expectations, the achieved assurance falls short of that required. Only if the sample results are better than expected can the achieved assurance match required assurance. This alternative creates many more instances where the auditor must conduct further audit work on the basis of a study of the errors in the sample. However, it has the advantage of causing the auditor to study the errors at an early stage.

No matter which approach is adopted, the basic principles of substantive test design remain the same, i.e.

(1) The assurance achieved from the substantive test depends upon
   (a) The method used to identify the population from which the representative sample is selected;
   (b) The method used to identify the population of key items;
   (c) The balance between the 'representative' and 'key item' samples;
   (d) The number of items selected;
   (e) The sample results actually obtained;
   (f) The quality of evidence available to substantiate key item and representative samples.
   The fifth factor (the sample results actually obtained) is outside the auditor's control, and may cause the assurance achieved from the substantive testing to fall short of the assurance required.
(2) If the assurance achieved does fall short of the assurance required, the auditor extends the substantive testing after a study of the errors discovered in the sample.

THE DEBTORS AUDIT

Assurance Received from Previous Audit Steps

Before commencing the substantive tests for debtors the auditor should decide the overall assurance required for debtors and the assurance already obtained from previously performed audit work. The three major categories of audit work which may have already generated assurance in the debtors figure are:

(1) Audit work performed on interrelated accounts;
(2) The results of analytical review procedures involving debtors;
(3) An assessment of any internal controls over debtors.

INTERRELATED ACCOUNTS

Figure 6.8 is a specimen debtors ledger control account showing the types of transactions or events which might typically result in movement in the debtors figure. Obtaining a month-by-month picture of movements on the debtors ledger is an important procedure in the 'population statistics' stage of the audit evidence process for debtors. It provides valuable planning information for the debtors audit. It is likely that the major movements in debtors will come from sales and cash receipts, and therefore assurance in the debtors figure will come from the audit of sales and cash receipts assuming that the audit of these transactions precedes the audit of debtors. It is useful to identify specific relationships between the detailed objectives of the sales and

Specimen debtors ledger control account			
Opening balance	a	Cash receipts	e
Sales	b	Discounts	f
Interest on overdue balances	c	Returns	g
Dishonoured cheques	d	Invoicing errors corrected	h
		Bad debts	i
		Other journal entries	j
		Closing balance	l
	x̄		x̄

Figure 6.8

cash receipts audits on the one hand, and the detailed objectives of the debtors audit on the other.

Sales validity: If an invalid sale is recorded as a debtor, then that recorded debtor does not *exist.* Invalid sales are not the only possible source of non-existent debtors, but if it can be established (with reasonable assurance) that only valid sales are recorded, the likelihood of non-existent debtors is reduced.

Sales completeness: If a sale is not recorded as a sale, it is likely that it will also be omitted from debtors. A failure to record a sale is not the only possible source of incomplete debtors, but if it can be established that recorded sales are complete, the likelihood of incomplete debtors is reduced.

Sales valuation: If a sale is incorrectly valued and posted to the debtors ledger then that debtors balance is also incorrectly valued. Incorrectly valued sales are not the only source of incorrectly valued debtors (another problem area is bad debts), but if it can be established that sales are correctly valued, the likelihood of incorrectly valued debtors is reduced.

Cash receipts validity: An invalid cash receipt recorded in the debtors ledger would cause an understatement of debtors. This could be regarded as either incompleteness of debtors or debtors being incorrectly valued. It follows that if it can be established that recorded cash receipts are valid, the likelihood of debtors being understated (through incompleteness/incorrect valuation) is reduced.

Cash receipts completeness: A failure to record a cash receipt causes a debtor to be shown when, in fact, the amount is paid. This could be regarded as either the recording of non-existent debtors or the recording of debtors at an incorrect value. If it can be established that cash receipts are complete, the likelihood of debtors being overstated (through non-existent debtors/incorrect valuation) is reduced.

Cash receipts valuation: A failure to record a cash receipt at the right amount causes debtors to be incorrectly valued. If it can be established that cash receipts are recorded for the right amount, the likelihood of debtors being incorrectly valued is reduced.

In addition to the results of the sales and cash receipts audits, the auditor should also pay attention to the results of audit investigations of the following items (where applicable) also related to debtors (see Figure 6.8):

Interest on overdue accounts
Dishonoured cheques
Discounts
Returns
Invoicing errors corrected
Bad debts written off
Other journal entries

Such audit investigations include:

(1) Finding Out the Enterprise's Policy and Procedures

For example:
What is the enterprise's policy on charging interest on overdue accounts, and is this agreed with the relevant customers?
What does the enterprise do when it receives a dishonoured cheque?
Is trading discontinued with the customer concerned, and is the possible bad debt write-off investigated?
What level of discount is allowed as part of the conditions of sale?
Who is reponsible for ensuring that
    (a) all discounts claimed by customers are allowable, and
    (b) all allowable discounts claimed by customers are recorded in the ledgers?
Who is responsible for ensuring that customers' complaints and debit notes are examined, and that
    (a) all justifiable credits are given, and
    (b) only justifiable credits are given?

What evidence is required of a sales return or invoicing error before credit is granted?

Who is responsible for ensuring that

    (a) all known bad debts are written off, and

    (b) only known bad debts are written off?

What evidence of a bad debt is required before the debt is written off?

What is the reason for any other journal entries, and upon whose authority are they made?

(2) Performing Relevant Analytical Reviews

For example:

Is the current relationship between discounts and sales in line with past experience?

Is the current relationship between bad debts written off and sales in line with past experience?

Is the current relationship between sales returns and sales in line with past experience?

(3) Performing Substantive Tests (if necessary)

The assurance required from the substantive tests depends on the significance of the matter under investigation, the result of relevant analytical reviews, and the appropriateness of the enterprise's own policy and procedures. For example, where discounts are a significant amount, discounts are a higher than usual level of sales, and the enterprise has not performed its own investigation of discounts, then the auditor is likely to want to substantively test the discounts given. If discounts are a small amount and they have the usual relationship to sales, the auditor may be justified in not performing any substantive tests.

ANALYTICAL REVIEW PROCEDURES

The principal analytical review procedures which directly involve debtors and can provide assurance in support of the debtors figure are:

(1) The relationship between debtors at the end of a period and sales for the period. At any point in time it is possible to calculate the number of days' sales included in debtors. The relationship between debtors and sales is frequently studied by examining the movement in the number of days' sales in debtors over a period of time. An otherwise unexpected increase in this statistic may indicate non-existent debtors (not matched by invalid sales) or a potential bad debts problem as a result of slower payments by customers.

(2) The relationship between debtors over a certain age and total debtors. At any point in time it is possible to age the debtors balances (typically, each debtors balance is analysed into amounts under 30 days old, amounts unpaid for between 30 and 60 days, 60 and 90 days, and over 90 days). It is then possible to calculate, for example, the percentage of debtors over 90 days old, and between 60 and 90 days old. Any increase in these two percentages over time may indicate old non-existent debtors or a potential bad debt problem.

One factor affecting the quality of analytical review procedures is the quality of the information from which relationships are observed over time. When a review procedure depends, for instance, upon ageing analyses of debtors, and those ageing analyses are performed by enterprise staff, it is desirable for the auditor to perform some detailed checks of the ageing analyses (by reference to the debtors ledgers) in order to be satisfied that the information upon which the analytical review is based is satisfactory.

INTERNAL CONTROLS

Internal controls over debtors, as opposed to sales and other accounts related to debtors, are generally confined to such procedures (performed by enterprise staff) as:

(1) Maintenance of debtors ledger control account and reconciliation with the sum of the individual debtors' balances.
(2) Review of ageing analyses and enquiry into long-outstanding debts.

The maintenance of the debtors ledger control account and its reconciliation with the debtors ledger is a most important internal control. A failure to reconcile may be caused by one or more of the following:

(a) Posting a transaction to a debtors ledger account at the wrong value, resulting in *incorrectly valued debtors.*
(b) Failure to post a transaction to a debtors ledger account, resulting in *incomplete debtors* (failure to post sales) or *non-existent debtors* (failure to post cash receipts).
(c) Failure to sum properly a class of transactions (sales, cash receipts, etc.) resulting in the transactions of that class being incorrectly summarised in the control account and the financial statements (*summation: transactions*).
(d) Failure to compute properly the balance on an individual debtor's account or failure to sum properly all the debtors' balances, resulting in the individual debtors being incorrectly summarised in the financial statements (*summation: debtors*).

It follows that a debtors ledger control account which reconciles provides some assurance for the following detailed objectives:

Debtors: valuation, completeness, existence, summation.
Transactions (sales, cash receipts, etc.): summation.

THE DEBTORS CIRCULARISATION

Typically, the main effort in the substantive testing of debtors is the *debtors circularisation*. A debtors circular is a letter addressed to a debtor of the enterprise under audit, drafted by the auditor but written on the enterprise's notepaper, and signed by enterprise management. In it, the enterprise asks its customer to use the circular to confirm, direct to the enterprise's auditor, the outstanding balance owed by the customer to the enterprise at a particular point in time (the confirmation date). The outstanding balance per the enterprise's records is usually stated in the circular.

Debtors circulars are sent to a sample of debtors, and the selection of this sample must be under the control of the auditor, who should ensure that:

(1) The representative component of the sample is selected from a complete listing of the debtors;
(2) The key item sample includes:
    (a) A selection of nil or low balances on accounts which have recently been active;

Auditor	Enterprise
(1) Drafts wording and format of circular	(2) Agrees wording and format
	(3) Blank circulars printed on enterprise's headed notepaper and signed by appropriate member of the enterprise's management team
(4) Selects representative and key item samples	(5) Agrees there is no objection to circularising the customers selected
(6) Details are entered on circulars and listed on a circularisation schedule	
(7) Circulars posted	
(8) Circulars returned direct to the auditor	(9) Enterprise is informed of circularisation results and investigates queries

Figure 6.9   Involvements of the enterprise and the auditor in debtors circularisation

(b) A selection of long-outstanding balances;

(c) A selection of high-value balances.

Once the sample is selected, the debtors circulars can be prepared, and again this detailed preparation should be under the control of the auditor. Details of circulars should be scheduled by the auditor, and finally the circulars should be posted by the auditor to avoid any possible management interference. The auditor then waits for the circulars to be returned from the enterprise's customers. Figure 6.9 indicates the typical involvement of the enterprise and the auditor in the debtors circularisation process up to the stage of the return of the circulars.

When the Circulars are Returned

If the circularisation produces a low response rate, the auditor may decide upon a second circularisation of non-respondents. All replies should be recorded in the circularisation schedule until either the flow of responses dries up, or time pressure requires further audit work to commence. The further audit work required falls into three areas:

(1) Further work required to respond to the differences revealed by the disagreed replies. (*Analysis of differences.*)

(2) Further work required to follow up the non-replies. (*Alternative procedures.*)

(3) Further work required since the debtors circularisation plus the analysis of differences (where appropriate) is not capable of providing sufficient evidence for certain debtors audit objectives. (*Supplementary procedures.*) Supplementary procedures may be carried out before the debtors circularisation.

(1) Analysis of differences

In each case where a difference is reported it must be investigated to discover whether the difference reflects a misstatement of the debtors balance or is the result of a routine timing difference. This investigation may either be conducted by the auditor or by the enterprise. If conducted by the enterprise, the findings must subsequently be substantiated by the auditor.

Common causes of differences between the customer and the enterprise are:

(a) *The customer claims that an invoice(s) has been paid:* this may be a routine timing difference, where the customer makes a payment before the confirmation date but the enterprise does not receive the payment until after the confirmation date. In this case, the debtors are not mis-stated.

Alternatively, the cause of the disagreement may be a cash receipts cut-off error or a theft of cash. In these cases debtors would be overstated.

(b) *The customer claims that the goods were not received:* this may be a routine timing difference, where the enterprise despatches the goods before the confirmation date but the customer receives the goods after the confirmation date. In this case, debtors are not mis-stated. Alternatively, the despatch may have gone astray or the despatch may have been recorded in the wrong time period by the enterprise. In these cases, debtors would be overstated.

(c) *The customer claims that the goods were returned:* this may be a routine timing difference, where the customer returns the goods before the confirmation date but the enterprise does not receive notice of the return of goods (and therefore issue a credit note) until after the confirmation date. Alternatively, the disagreement may indicate a failure to issue a credit note promptly. Although in either case the debtors should be adjusted, the second case is more likely to be indicative of a widespread problem, since the number of instances of timing problems of the kind described in the first case should be limited.

(d) *The customer claims that there is an error in the price charged, that the goods were damaged, or that the proper quantity of goods was not received:* clerical errors and disputes are the most common cause of differences. The circumstances should be investigated to determine whether the enterprise is in error, and, if so, the size of the error.

Figure 6.10 provides a summary of the type of audit error which may be associated with each type of circularisation difference. It follows that where a balance is agreed by a debtor or that the difference is established as a routine timing difference, then the returned circular contributes to the detailed objectives of debtors cut-off, existence and valuation.

Confirmation difference	Error in debtors account
(1) Payment made by the customer	(a) Cut-off (b) Existence (theft of cash)
(2) Goods not received by the customer	(a) Cut-off (b) Existence (goods gone astray)
(3) Goods returned	(a) Cut-off (b) Existence
(4) Clerical errors and disputed amounts	(a) Valuation

Figure 6.10

(2) Alternative procedures

For those debtors who fail to return the debtors circular the auditor must perform alternative procedures to obtain the assurance otherwise obtained from the returned circular. The following evidence can be examined as an alternative to the debtors circular:

(a) *Cash receipts:* subsequent cash receipts which can be clearly identified with the outstanding balance at the confirmation date provide high-quality evidence as to the existence, ownership and valuation of the debtor.
(b) *Copy sales invoices:* these are useful as evidence of the existence of sales invoices contained in the debtor's balance.
(c) *Despatch note:* these evidence the despatch of goods.
(d) *Correspondence between the enterprise and the debtor:* this may be reviewed by the auditor in cases where the debtors balance is in dispute.

(3) Supplementary procedures

It can be seen from Figure 6.10 that the debtors circularisation is capable of detecting differences which are the result of cut-off and certain existence and valuation errors in the debtors account. However, it is not capable of detecting errors of ownership, classification and disclosure. In addition, circularisation is not a satisfactory technique for detecting the omission of account balances in debtors (incompleteness) and the realisable value of debtors (valuation). In all these cases, the possibility of error must be investigated by procedures other than the debtors circularisation.

Incompleteness – Omission of Account Balances

It is extremely difficult to test for omitted account balances in the listing of debtors. The principal sources of assurance are:

(a) Debtors ledger control account balance reconciles with the total of the listing of debtors. This provides assurance that a debtor with a balance in the debtors ledger is not omitted from the debtors listing.
(b) Nil balances included in the debtors circularisation are returned agreed. This provides assurance that debtors excluded from the debtors listing by virture of being nil value are properly valued.
(c) Tests for incompleteness of sales. If it can be established that recorded sales are complete, the likelihood of incomplete debtors is reduced.

Valuation – Net Realisable Value

It is usual for the auditor to evaluate the adequacy of the bad debts provision through a study of the long-outstanding debtors balances in the ageing list of debtors. If this work has already been performed by the enterprise staff, the auditor's own study may be reduced if its results support the conclusions of the enterprise's investigation.

Ownership

The debtors may have been factored, and, if so, this is unlikely to be discovered through the debtors circularisation. Evidence of factoring may be found in the enterprise's minutes, management representations, correspondence files, etc.

Classification/Disclosure

The auditor should scrutinise the debtors listing to ensure that any amounts which should be shown separately from trade debtors (e.g. amounts receivable from directors, subsidiaries) are shown separately.

THE QUALITY OF DEBTORS CIRCULARS AS AUDIT EVIDENCE

It was stated earlier in this chapter that 'where a balance is agreed by a debtor or the difference is established as a routine timing difference, then the returned circular contributes to the detailed objectives of debtors cut-off, existence and valuation'. It should be noticed, however, that the results of recent experimental studies have brought into question the effectiveness of debtors circulars in contributing to these objectives. For example, one recent American experiment[1] examined the effectiveness of circulars by deliberately circularising the instalment loan account customers of a bank with incorrect balances. Of those that responded by returning the circulars, it was found that 54 per cent confirmed the incorrect balance and only 46 per cent detected the error. An abstract from the results is reproduced as Figure 6.11, and it is seen that, whilst the average detection rate is 46 per cent, the detection rate does vary depending upon whether:

(1) The error is small or large, and
(2) Whether the error causes the true figure to be understated or overstated.

Negative and extended field circulars

The type of circular which asks the customer to respond whether or not the customer agrees with the balance shown in the circular is called a *positive circular*. There is another type of circular used in practice which only asks the customer to respond if the customer disagrees the balance. This type of circular is called a *negative circular*. The same experiment using the loan

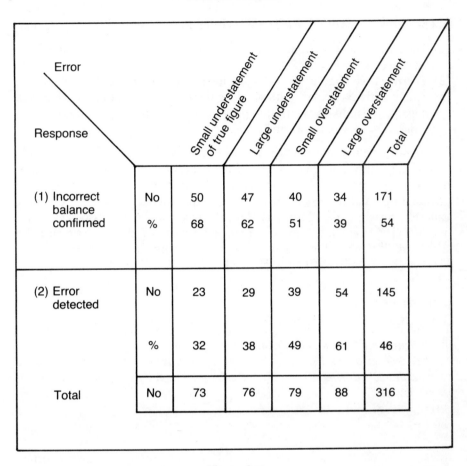

Error Response		Small understatement of true figure	Large understatement	Small overstatement	Large overstatement	Total
(1) Incorrect balance confirmed	No	50	47	40	34	171
	%	68	62	51	39	54
(2) Error detected	No	23	29	39	54	145
	%	32	38	49	61	46
Total	No	73	76	79	88	316

Figure 6.11

instalment account customers of a bank tested the effectiveness of negative circulars. It was found that of 415 customers deliberately circularised (using the negative form) with incorrect balances, only 74 replied to point out the error. This gave a detection rate as low as 18 per cent.

The same experiment also tested a novel form of circular, not presently used in practice to a significant extent, called the *extended field circular*. In this the enterprise's customer is asked to circle one of three stated balances (one of which is the balance per the enterprise's records) and to return the circular to the auditor. In both the positive and negative forms of circular the customer is quoted only one balance – the balance per the enterprise's records. The experimental tests of the expanded field circular indicated a detection rate of 89 per cent – far in excess of the positive circular (46 per cent) or the negative circular (18 per cent).

The implications of this experiment for the use of debtors circulars are that:

(1) The extended field circular is an interesting suggestion, possibly worthy of adoption in practice.
(2) The negative circular provides relatively little assurance for the auditor.
(3) The positive circular, although significantly more effective than the negative, is unlikely by itself to provide sufficient assurance of those audit objectives to which it contributes.

One possible limitation on the results of this experiment is the fact that the loan instalment account customers of the bank were all individuals. Perhaps business enterprises take more care than individuals before confirming outstanding balances. Nevertheless, such experiments are capable of giving valuable insights into assurance levels which should be associated with debtors circulars. Based on the reported results of this experiment, the suspicion is that auditors may presently be taking more assurance from debtors circularisations than is justified.

REFERENCE

1. Horton L. Sorkin, *Third Party Confirmation Requests: A New Approach Utilizing an Expanded Field,* published in *Auditing Symposium IV; Proceedings of the 1978 Touche Ross/University of Kansas Symposium on Auditing Problems* (School of Business, University of Kansas, 1979), pp. 61–72.

7 Planning, Controlling and Recording

PLANNING

An important part of the audit planning is the selection by the auditor of the best 'approach' to the audit. The audit evidence process suggested in this book is a logical order in which to collect and evaluate audit evidence, but the logical order does not indicate the *emphasis* which should be given to the various steps in the audit evidence process. The auditor must obtain sufficient overall assurance from all audit steps to support the audit opinion, but the extent to which assurance is derived from any one audit step can be varied, within limits, by adjusting the extent to which each audit step is utilised and developed in the audit plan.

If the auditor decides to give particular emphasis to one step in the audit process it is frequently said that a particular approach to the audit is being adopted. For example, emphasis on the study of the accounting systems and its internal controls is referred to as the 'systems' approach. Emphasis on the detailed substantive testing is a 'substantive' approach, etc. It is most desirable that a firm of auditors does not develop standard procedures which require, for every audit, the adoption of the same particular approach. The circumstances of each enterprise are different, and the auditor should select the most suitable approach for those circumstances. Moreover, within the same enterprise audit, the approach selected for one balance sheet or transactions area may be different from that selected for another area.

Typical decisions that the auditor has to make in planning the audit approach are:

(1) Whether to emphasise the study of the accounting system and its internal controls *or* to emphasise the detailed substantive testing. The fact that the auditor may not wish to emphasise the study of internal control is recognised in paragraph 5 of the Auditor's Operational Standard, which opens with the words '*If* the auditor wishes to place reliance on any internal controls . . .' and in paragraph 7 of the Auditing Guideline on Planning, Controlling and Recording, which states 'the auditor should consider the outline audit approach he proposes to adopt, including the extent to which he *may wish* to rely on internal controls . . .'.

(2) If emphasis is given to the accounting system and its internal controls, whether to perform any detailed substantive tests of balance sheet items at the interim audit (i.e. during the accounting period) *or* at the final audit (i.e. at the end of the accounting period).
(3) If emphasis is given to the detailed substantive tests, whether to emphasise substantive tests of transactions *or* substantive tests of balance sheet items.

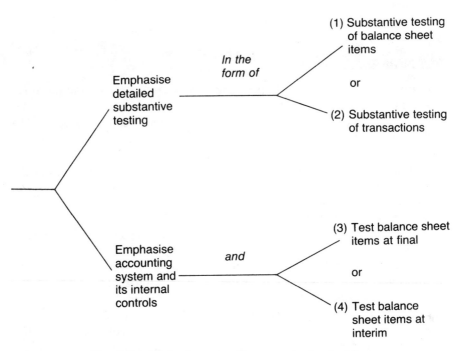

Figure 7.1   Selecting an audit approach: the decisions

Figure 7.1 puts these essential decisions in the form of a decision tree, whereas Figure 7.2 illustrates the four alternative approaches (the four outcomes) implied by such a decision process. Audit steps above the jagged line are conducted at the interim audit and those below the line at the final audit. The size of the blocks indicates the emphasis given to each audit step under each alternative. These blocks represent inputs in terms of audit time and effort rather than outputs in the form of assurance contributed by each audit step. It is assumed that in all four cases the total assurance achieved is the same and is sufficient to support the same audit opinion. It is not necessarily the case, however, that the four audit approaches involve the same total sum of audit time and effort.

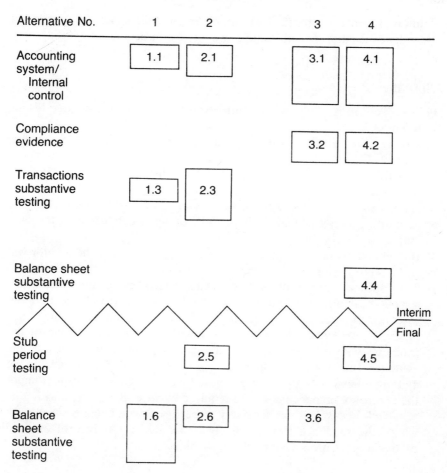

Figure 7.2 Alternative audit approaches

Alternative 1

(1) The decision is taken to concentrate on balance sheet substantive testing as shown by the size of block 1.6 (Figure 7.2).

(2) It is necessary to perform some substantive testing of transactions (block 1.3) on specific detailed audit objectives where balance sheet testing is inefficient. For example, it is difficult to devise balance sheet tests which provide all the assurance required regarding the incompleteness of debtors, and, to satisfy this objective, it may be necessary to test also the incompleteness of sales.

(3) If it is necessary to perform some transactions substantive testing, it is also necessary to make a related study of the accounting system and its

internal controls (block 1.1), in order to understand the quality of evidence used in the substantive testing of transactions.

Alternative 2

(1) The decision is taken to concentrate on transactions substantive testing (block 2.3).
(2) This requires a related study of the accounting system and its internal controls (block 2.1).
(3) The transactions testing performed at the interim audit must be supplemented by some testing (stub period testing – block 2.5) of transactions for the period between the interim audit and the end of the accounting period. Such 'stub period' testing is conducted at the final audit.
(4) It is likely, given the transactions testing approach, that the auditor will still wish to perform a small measure of balance sheet testing (block 2.6). This follows from one of the basic factors which lies behind the auditor's selection of audit evidence – the need to strike a balance between evidence the creation of which is largely under the control of the enterprise and evidence whose creation lies with third parties. One of the problems with over-reliance on transactions testing is that much of the evidence (e.g. order, despatch, copy sales invoice) upon which the auditor relies is processed or generated by the accounting system under the control of management. The required balance, therefore, may not be achieved, and it may be necessary to perform some balance sheet work where the evidence is more likely to be under the control of third parties (e.g. debtors confirmations, bank certificates).

Alternative 3

(1) The decision is taken to concentrate on the accounting system and its internal controls as a source of audit evidence (block 3.1).
(2) Related compliance evidence must be obtained (block 3.2), preferably in the form of inspection of written evidence of performance (compliance tests). The Auditor's Operational Standard states: 'If the auditor wishes to place reliance on any internal controls he should ascertain and evaluate those controls *and perform compliance tests on their operation*.'[1]
(3) Given the limitations of internal control as a source of audit evidence, some substantive evidence would normally be performed to support the study of internal controls. The Auditing Guideline on Internal Controls states: 'Because of the inherent limitations in even the most effective internal control system, it will not be possible for the auditor to rely solely on its operation as a basis for his opinion on the financial statements.'[2]

The illustration given in Figure 7.2 supports internal control with detailed substantive testing of balance sheet items (block 3.6), although some substantive testing of transactions may also be appropriate.

(4) It may be desirable to perform some stub period compliance tests, although, provided that the stub period is shorter than the turnover period for balance sheet items, most errors occurring in the stub period should be capable of discovery in the balance sheet testing.

Alternative 4

(1) The decision is taken to concentrate on the accounting system and its internal controls as a source of audit evidence (block 4.1). Once again, compliance evidence is necessary (block 4.2), preferably in the form of inspection of written evidence of performance (compliance tests).

(2) Further substantive testing is necessary, and it has been decided to perform substantive balance sheet tests at the interim audit (i.e. prior to the end of the accounting period – block 4.4).

(3) It is necessary to perform stub period testing (block 4.5), which may either be further compliance testing or substantive tests of stub period transactions, to cover the fact that neither the original compliance test nor the balance sheet test would pick up errors occurring in the stub period. It is likely that a small amount of balance sheet substantive testing will still be required at the year-end (for example, reconciliation of the cash book balance with the bank certificate). However, this small amount of year-end substantive work is not represented on Figure 7.2.

The four alternatives given in Figure 7.2 are obviously not the only possibilities from which the auditor can choose, but they illustrate the major problems involved.

Stub Period Testing

The importance of stub period testing is recognised by the Auditing Guideline on Internal Controls which states:

'If reliance is to be placed on the operation of controls the auditor should ensure that there is evidence of the effectiveness of those controls throughout the whole period under review. Compliance tests carried out at an interim date prior to the year end need, therefore, to be supplemented by tests of controls for the remainder of the year; alternatively, the auditor will need to carry out other procedures to enable him to gain adequate assurance as to the reliability of the accounting records during the period which has not been subject to compliance tests.'[3]

FACTORS DETERMINING THE SELECTION OF THE AUDIT APPROACH

The principal factors determining the selection of the audit approach are:

(a) The quality of audit evidence *available* from each audit step.

For example, if the enterprise's accounting system has few internal controls, or compliance evidence is unavailable, then the quality of internal control as a source of audit evidence may be low, and, if so, this is a major factor in reducing the emphasis given to this particular audit step.

(b) The quality of planning information available from each audit step.

For example, a study of the accounting system and its internal controls provides an understanding of the quality of documentary evidence processed or generated by the system. If this information is valuable to the substantive testing of transactions, then the emphasis given to the accounting system is increased.

(c) The cost of obtaining audit evidence/planning information from each audit step.

(d) The quality of audit staff available.

The auditor cannot select an audit approach dependent upon sophisticated analytical review, statistical sampling or computer audit techniques if staff with the necessary understanding and experience of the techniques are unavailable.

(e) Timing of the availability of audit staff.

The auditor must select an audit approach where the audit staff are available at the time the audit work is due to be performed. This time varies according to the audit approach, and this gives the auditor some room for manoeuvre. For example, an approach requiring interim audit work may be selected because staff are available at that time rather than at the end of the accounting period.

(f) The timing of the audit report.

Audit approaches which require a minimum of audit work at the final audit are desirable if the audit report and the financial statements are to be issued by the enterprise as soon as possible after the end of the accounting period.

(g) The timing of the availability of audit evidence and information supporting the financial statements. For example:

(1) When is the stocktake to be held? It may not be possible to adopt an approach which substantively tests stock before the end of the accounting period if the enterprise's stocktake is at the end of the period.

(2) Which schedules supporting the financial statements are to be produced by the enterprise, and when will they be available?

AUDIT PLANNING AS A FEATURE THROUGHOUT THE AUDIT

The audit evidence process itself provides the auditor with an outline plan of the *sequence* of events. In the first instance, the auditor should also prepare an *outline plan* of the *emphasis* to be given to each audit step in the process. To a large extent this outline is based on knowledge of the enterprise derived from previous audits. After each step in the audit process has been performed, the auditor revises his plans for the remaining stages on the basis of all the information obtained to date. For example, if the auditor has reached the stage at which the study of the accounting system and internal controls is

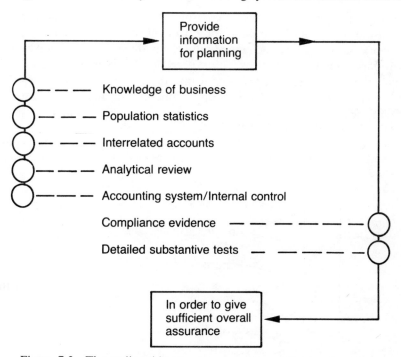

Figure 7.3   The audit evidence process and the audit planning process

complete (Figure 7.3), then he should use all information derived from the knowledge of business, population statistics, interrelated accounts, analytical review and internal control steps of the audit process in order to plan the compliance and detailed substantive testing, so that the assurance expected from all steps in the audit process provides sufficient evidence to support the audit opinion.

It follows that there are seven important points in the audit planning process when the auditor may have to revise the plans or form more definite plans for the remainder of the audit. Each one of these points corresponds to the completion of a step in the audit evidence process. In effect, audit planning does not occur once at the beginning of the audit but continues throughout the audit. The importance of planning throughout the audit is recognised in the Auditing Guideline on Planning, Controlling and Recording, which states that 'in order to ensure that an audit is carried out effectively and efficiently, the work needs to be planned, controlled and recorded at each stage of its progress'.[4]

CONTROL AS A FEATURE THROUGHOUT THE AUDIT

'The most important elements of control of an audit are the direction and supervision of the audit staff and the review of the work they have done.'[5] 'The work performed by each member of the audit staff is reviewed by more senior persons in the audit firm. This is necessary to ensure that the work was adequately performed and to confirm that the results obtained support the audit conclusions which have been reached.'[6] In particular, wherever planning decisions are being made or revised by junior staff they should, ideally, be reviewed by more senior staff before the next step in the audit process is performed. Such procedures would result in ten review points including (Figure 7.4):

Figure 7.4   The review points

(1) A review of the outline audit plan at the outset;
(2) A review of each of the seven steps of the audit process;
(3) A review of the review of the financial statements; and
(4) A review of the audit report.

A Review of the Outline Audit Plan

The review of the outline audit plan should involve the partner in charge of the audit, and should be performed before the detailed audit work commences. Such partner-involvement at the beginning of the audit can be very valuable in ensuring that an efficient approach acceptable to the partner in charge is selected. It should not, however, inhibit changes being made to the outline plan in response to changed circumstances discovered during the audit. Following completion of the review of the outline plan all field staff should be briefed as to the plan's contents.

A Review of Each of the Seven Steps of the Audit Process

Normally, these reviews would be conducted by senior field staff immediately after completion of each audit step. If, as a consequence of the results of an audit step, a significant deviation from the outline plan is considered desirable, then senior field staff should consult with the manager or partner for the audit. There should always be open and easy *communication* between all those involved in the audit. In particular, senior field staff should have access to the manager and partner for early discussion of problems encountered.

Although the reviews of the results of each audit step are conducted by senior field staff in the first instance, there should be further review of these results by the manager and partner at the end of the interim and/or final audits.

A Review of the Review of the Financial Statements

A review of the financial statements is most important where the required audit opinion is whether or not the financial statements give a true and fair view. To a significant extent the review is judgmental, since it involves an assessment as to whether the financial statements as a whole give a true and fair view and are a reflection of the underlying economic circumstances of the enterprise. Although some aspects of the review of the financial statements, such as compliance with statutory and other regulations, can be performed without the significant exercise of judgment, an overall assessment of the financial statements must be conducted by an experienced person, such as the partner in charge. It follows that the review of the review of the financial statements must be performed by an equally experienced person, and a second partner may be required to perform this function.

The Auditing Guideline on Planning, Controlling and Recording recognises the possibility of second-partner involvement in the context of the resolution of matters of principle or contentious matters:

'Where matters of principle or contentious matters arise which may affect the audit opinion the auditor should consider consulting another experienced accountant. This accountant may be a partner, a senior colleague or another practitioner.'[7]

A Review of the Audit Report

It is desirable that a second partner should in any event read the draft audit report to approve the form of wording, especially if the report is qualified. The audit report is the only part of the annual report and financial statements which is prepared by the auditor rather than the enterprise. Any mistakes therein reflect particularly badly upon the auditor.

The review concept might be extended to include:

(1) Review by the internal auditing department of the audit firm of the firm's procedures and of the application of those procedures to specific audits (i.e. compliance).
(2) A peer review whereby the review of the firm's procedures and compliance therewith is conducted by another auditing firm, which issues either a private or public report of its findings. At the time of writing such peer reviews have been restricted to the United States.
(3) A review of the audit firm's procedures as applied to a particular enterprise by the audit committee of that enterprise.
(4) As part of an investigation by Department of Trade Inspectors into the affairs of an enterprise, those Inspectors may investigate the audit of the enterprise concerned.
(5) Auditing procedures may be reviewed by a court of law in any action for negligence against an auditing firm.

It is clear that ultimately the review process can extend beyond the boundaries of the audit firm itself to include review by third parties. Although such an extension may not be commonplace, the audit firm should be prepared for such an eventuality.

THE ROLE OF WORKING PAPERS

The objectives of working papers are:

(1) To provide a means of *communication*. The outline plan and the detailed audit work to be performed can be communicated from senior to junior staff by means of working papers. The results of the audit work, including

any problems encountered, are communicated from junior to senior staff by the same means. Auditor's working papers should provide an adequate record of the work that has been carried out and the conclusions that have been reached. Communication should not be restricted to working papers, which should be supported by oral explanation. Nevertheless, the immediate recording of the results of audit work helps the auditor's memory to cope with what can be a significant delay between the conduct of the work and the review. Thus the Auditing Guideline recommends that auditor's working papers should be prepared as the audit proceeds so that details and problems are not omitted.

It should be further remembered that working papers provide a means of communication with those conducting the audit in future accounting periods. Results of prior audits is a most important source of knowledge of the business.

(2) To provide a form of *evidence*. Working papers provide, for future reference, evidence of work performed and conclusions drawn therefrom in arriving at the audit opinion. From the point of view of junior staff it is important to provide supervisory staff with evidence of the performance of work. From the point of view of the auditing firm such evidence may be necessary if the audit is reviewed by a third party. The Auditing Guideline suggests that working papers should be prepared to the following standard:

> 'Audit working papers should always be sufficiently complete and detailed to enable an experienced auditor with no previous connection with the audit subsequently to ascertain from them what work was performed and to support the conclusions reached.'[8]

(3) To provide a form of *discipline*. The requirement to prepare working papers encourages the person carrying out the audit work to adopt a methodical approach both to the conduct of the audit work and to the logic applied in reaching conclusions. The auditor is forced, in setting out the working papers, to justify the conclusions reached on the basis of the results of the audit work. If the conclusions of junior staff are overturned by more senior staff, the reasoning must be particularly well explained. The Auditing Guideline states:

> 'If difficult questions of principle or of judgment arise, the auditor should record the relevant information received and summarise both the management's and his conclusions. It is in such areas as these that the auditor's judgment may subsequently be questioned, particularly by a third party who has the benefit of hindsight. It is important to be able to tell what facts were known at the time the auditor reached his conclusion and to be able to demonstrate that, based on those facts, the conclusion was reasonable.'[9]

In order to be able to demonstrate the reasonableness of the conclusion to third parties, the auditor must first demonstrate its reasonableness to himself: thus working papers promote self-discipline.

WORKING PAPERS AS A FEATURE THROUGHOUT THE AUDIT

Audit work performed should be recorded as soon as possible after performance, and, in any event, working papers relating to one step in the audit evidence process should be completed (including a record of conclusions drawn) before the auditor proceeds to the next step in the process. The basic information contained in the working papers is expressed in different forms depending on the step in the process to which the working paper relates. For example:

(1) *Knowledge of business:* Basic information is in descriptive narrative form. The working papers containing the narrative description are generally kept on a 'permanent' file, which is distinct from the 'current' audit file. The permanent file is updated every accounting period and referred to on each accounting period's audit. The current audit file contains information of primary value to the current period's audit, although information on the current audit file also provides an important source of reference to those performing the next period's audit. Working papers on the current audit file should specify the use made of the auditor's knowledge of the business in planning the current audit.

(2) *Population statistics:* Basic information is in the form of breakdown schedules and analyses. Where breakdown schedules are bulky it may be appropriate to keep them on a special file distinct from the current audit file (and permanent file). For example, a debtors listing used to record a circularisation might, together with the circulars returned, be kept in a special file. Working papers on the current audit file should specify the use made of population statistics in planning the audit.

(3) *Interrelated accounts:* All possible interrelationships between accounts can be listed, probably in matrix form, as a checklist available to the auditor. Working papers on the current audit file should specify those relationships used by the auditor in the current audit.

(4) *Analytical review:* Basic information is in the form of an analysis. Working papers should specify the information on which the analysis is based, the results of the analysis and the auditor's interpretation of those results.

An analytical review should also be performed as part of the review of financial statements (in addition to its role as part of the audit evidence process). It is general practice for large auditing firms to have a standard schedule demonstrating trends in key relationships over a number of years. The working papers should explain the interpretation which is made of such trends by those performing the review of financial statements.

(5) *Accounting system and its internal controls:* The basic information of the accounting system may be contained in a flowchart or in narrative notes. Details of the internal controls within the accounting system may be contained in an internal control questionnaire or in narrative notes. An internal control questionnaire is a list of questions designed to assist the auditor in the identification of internal controls within an accounting system. Many auditing firms use internal control questionnaires as part of their standard documentation. It is often convenient to keep the details of the accounting system and its internal controls in the permanent file or in a file of its own known as the 'systems' file. These details are updated and referred to during each accounting period's audit. The current audit file should contain details of the use made of internal controls in the current audit both as evidence (to be supported by compliance tests if possible) and as planning information for the substantive tests. The specific internal controls relied upon should be identified and their evaluation as audit evidence explained.

(6) *Compliance tests:* Working papers on the current audit file should specify:

(a) The object of the test (linked to an internal control to be relied upon).

(b) The audit evidence used in the test (including an evaluation of that evidence as evidence of compliance).

(c) The results.

(d) The interpretation placed upon those results.

(7) *Substantive tests:* A suggested format for a working paper covering substantive tests was given in Chapter 6, Figure 6.1. It contained details of:

(a) The object of the test (the assurance required in the validity of sales).

(b) The method of sample selection.

(c) The evidence employed.

(d) The results.

(e) The interpretation placed upon those results (the assurance achieved).

Working papers covering substantive tests should be on the current audit file.

The final stages of the audit

The final stages of the audit, including the review of financial statements, require special attention. It is at this stage of the audit, with pressures to finish the audit building for both partners and staff concerned, that relevant matters are most likely to be overlooked. An audit completion checklist helps to ensure that no routine procedures are overlooked. The preparation of a schedule summarising significant problems encountered during the audit helps to ensure that no difficult or unusual problems are left unresolved.

A REVIEW

Figure 7.5 serves to review the points made in this chapter. The *outline audit plan* is the outcome of the following four factors:

(1) *The enterprise's requirements:* the auditor must know the enterprise's plans in respect of such matters as:
   (a) Deadlines – when does the enterprise wish the audit to be completed?
   (b) Production of supporting schedules to the financial statements.
   (c) Provision of accounting, as opposed to auditing, services by the auditor.
   (d) Availability of audit evidence.
(2) *Auditing standards:* the outline audit plan should take account of the enterprise's requirements but these requirements should never be allowed to prejudice the technical auditing standards to which the audit must be performed.
(3) *Audit staff availability:* the auditor must plan within the limitations imposed by audit staff availability. Staff of suitable experience and competence must be available at the times required by the audit plan.
(4) *Prior knowledge:* the auditor plans the approach to the collection and evaluation of audit evidence on the basis of past experience (prior knowledge) of the enterprise. For example, if good systems have operated in the past, the auditor will expect to be able to rely on internal control as a source of evidence, and the systems approach may be adopted.

The audit plan and the budget

The audit plan outlines the component steps of the process of collecting and evaluating evidence (the audit evidence process), and it outlines the emphasis to be given to the audit steps in that process. The audit plan is the 'technical' plan, and it must be translated into a budget or 'commercial' plan on the basis of:
(a) Grade of staff required;
(b) Time needed;
(c) Pay rates;
(d) Overhead recovery rates.

Records of work and time

As a prerequisite to review it is vital that records are kept of
(a) The audit plan;

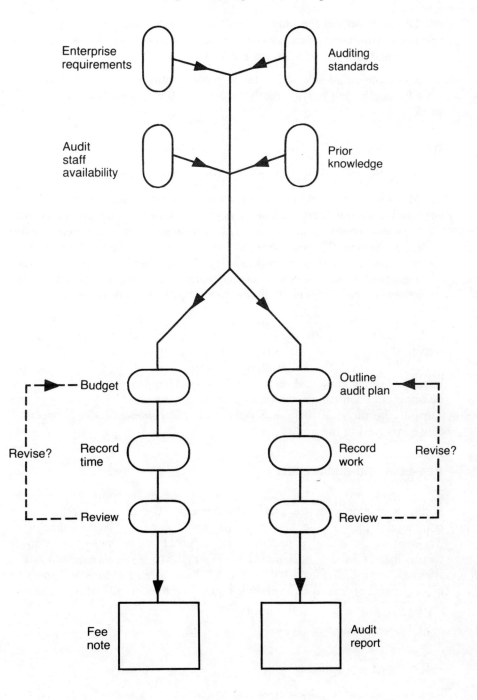

Figure 7.5

(b) The logic behind the plan;
(c) The performance of the plan including audit work undertaken, the results obtained and the conclusions reached.

On the commercial side it is vital to record both the budget and the time actually taken, and costs actually incurred in the performance of the audit work.

Review

Review is an essential ingredient of control. On the technical side:

(a) The audit plan should be reviewed by senior staff and a partner.
(b) The results obtained from audit work should be regularly compared with the logic behind the audit plan to see if the results indicate a need to revise the audit plan. This comparison is undertaken in the first instance by field staff, and is reviewed periodically during the audit by senior staff and/or a partner. In large audits a second partner may also be involved in the review process, especially if any difficult problems are revealed.

On the commercial side, costs incurred should be regularly compared against budget, and any significant variances investigated. Any need to revise the technical plan will create a corresponding need to revise the budget.

It is important to realise that planning does not happen once at the beginning of the audit and that control does not happen once at the end. Both planning and control are continuing features throughout the audit, and this can only be the case if there is open and easy *communication* between all those involved in the audit.

Fee note and audit report

The ultimate product of the technical plan is the audit report expressing the auditor's opinion upon the financial statements. The ultimate product of the commercial plan is the 'fee note' or invoice and subsequent receipt of payment for the technical product. The technical side of the audit (i.e. those factors listed on the right-hand side of Figure 7.5) and the commercial side of the audit (those factors listed on the left-hand side of Figure 7.5) must be co-ordinated. It is no use developing a plan which meets all technical requirements but neglects the commercial constraints, and vice versa.

REFERENCES

1. Auditing Standard 101, *The Auditor's Operational Standard*, para. 5.
2. Auditing Guideline 204, *Internal Controls*, para. 8.
3. *Ibid*, para. 17.
4. Auditing Guideline 201, *Planning, Controlling and Recording*, para. 2.
5. *Ibid*, para. 13.
6. *Ibid*, para. 14.
7. *Ibid*, para. 16.
8. *Ibid*, para. 19.
9. *Ibid*, para. 20.

Index